# Ring Around the Moon

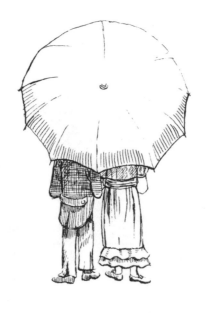

# Ring Around the Moon

## by Edith Fowke

*illustrated by Judith Gwyn Brown*

Prentice-Hall, Inc., Englewood Cliffs, New Jersey

RING AROUND THE MOON by Edith Fowke

Copyright © 1977 by Edith Fowke

First American edition published 1977 by Prentice-Hall, Inc.,
Englewood Cliffs, New Jersey.

10 9 8 7 6 5 4 3 2 1

**Library of Congress Cataloging in Publication Data**

Main entry under title:

Ring around the moon.

   Bibliography: p.
   Includes index.
   SUMMARY: A compilation of North American children's
rhymes, poems, and songs.
   1. Children's poetry, American. 2. Children's songs.
[1. American poetry—Collections. 2. Songs]
I. Fowke, Edith Fulton, 1913-    II. Brown, Judith Gwyn.
PZ8.3.R477        811'.008        76-44207
ISBN 0-13-781252-3

# Contents

# Introduction

My first collection of children's lore, *Sally Go Round the Sun*, contained singing games, skipping, ball-bouncing and clapping rhymes, foot and finger plays, counting-out rhymes, and taunts and teases – the kind of chants that are heard on every playground, and circulate among children between the ages of about five and eleven. This book is designed for slightly older children and presents a somewhat different type of lore: riddles, rounds, tongue twisters, animal songs, endless songs, charms and omens, answer-back songs, and verses about love and marriage. It has more and longer songs, and fewer short verses.

While the items in *Sally Go Round the Sun* were nearly all rhymes that children learned from other children, quite a few of those in *Ring Around the Moon* are songs that children learn from adults. Some fall into the large category of camp songs which are on the border between folk and popular: camp counsellors usually teach them to children in the first place, but then they pass into oral tradition when other children learn them from the first group.

Like the rhymes in *Sally Go Round the Sun*, all the items in *Ring Around the Moon* have been in oral tradition in Canada. Most of them came originally from the British Isles, some drifted up from the United States, and a few were composed here. Nearly all are in common use in other parts of the English-speaking world, and the section on "Sources and References" at the back of the book indicates who provided the particular versions given and where other similar items may be found.

I am grateful to the many people who contributed the rhymes and songs in this collection. These include children of friends, the Grade Three classes in various Toronto schools, and adults like Mrs. LaRena Clark, Mrs. Arlington

Fraser, Miss Alice Kane, Miss Claire McCausland, Mrs. Isabel Smaller, Mrs. Nellie Webb, and Lamont Tilden, who all contributed songs remembered from their own childhoods, and some they had heard from others with whom they came in contact. Roger Abrahams made available to me riddles that Timy Baranoff had heard in her childhood in Toronto. Five songs, "Mary Had a William Goat", "The Fox and the Goose", "A Leg of Mutton Went Over to France", "The Mallard", and "My Father Gave Me", are reprinted from Kenneth Peacock's *Songs of the Newfoundland Outports*, National Museum of Canada, Bulletin 197, and are reproduced by permission of Information Canada. "Sandy and the Mill" and "The Bagman" are reprinted from the *Journal of American Folklore*, 31(1918), 158, by permission of the American Folklore Society.

I must again express my gratitude to Keith Macmillan for his skilful transcription of the tunes from various tapes, and his transpositions of some of them to keys suitable for children.

I have been delighted to find that many children have taken *Sally Go Round the Sun* to their hearts, and I hope that this second volume will give them equal pleasure.

EDITH FOWKE

# Rounds

## 1.  Three Blind Mice

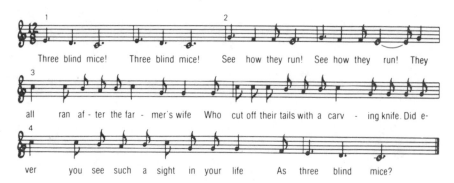

Three blind mice!  Three blind mice!  See how they run!  See how they run!  They
all   ran af - ter the far - mer's wife  Who  cut off their tails with a carv  -  ing knife. Did e-
ver   you see such a sight in your life   As   three   blind   mice?

Three blind mice! Three blind mice!
See how they run! See how they run!
They all ran after the farmer's wife
Who cut off their tails with a carving knife.
Did ever you see such a sight in your life
As three blind mice?

## 2.  Row, Row, Row your Boat

Row,   row,   row   your boat   Gent - ly   down   the   stream.
Mer - ri - ly, mer - ri - ly, mer - ri - ly, mer - ri - ly, Life   is   but   a   dream.

Row, row, row your boat
Gently down the stream.
Merrily, merrily, merrily, merrily,
Life is but a dream.

### 3. Frère Jacques

Are you sleep - ing, are you sleep - ing, Bro - ther John, Bro - ther John?

Morn-ing bells are ring - ing, morn-ing bells are ring - ing, Ding ding dong! Ding ding dong!

**A**

Frère Jacques, Frère Jacques,
Dormez-vous, dormez-vous?
Sonnez les matines, sonnez les matines,
Ding din don! Ding din don!

**B**

Are you sleeping, are you sleeping,
Brother John, Brother John?
Morning bells are ringing, morning bells are ringing,
Ding ding dong! Ding ding dong!

### 4. O How Lovely is the Evening

O how love - ly is the e - ve - ning, is the eve - ning, When to rest the

birds are steal - ing, bells are peal - ing, Ding dong, Ding dong, Ding dong.

O how lovely is the evening, is the evening,
When to rest the birds are stealing, bells are pealing,
Ding dong, ding dong, ding dong.

## 5. O Hark I Hear Those Pealing Bells

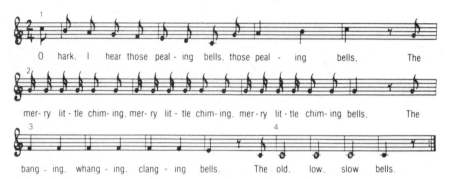

O hark, I hear those peal- ing bells, those peal - ing bells, The

mer- ry lit - tle chim- ing, mer- ry lit - tle chim- ing, mer- ry lit - tle chim- ing bells. The

bang - ing, whang - ing, clang - ing bells. The old, low, slow bells.

O hark, I hear those pealing bells, those pealing bells,
The merry little chiming, merry little chiming, merry little
    chiming bells,
The banging, whanging, clanging bells,
The old, low, slow bells.

## 6. Merrily, Merrily Greet the Morn

Mer - ri - ly, mer - ri - ly greet the morn, Chee - ri - ly, chee- ri - ly Sound the horn.

Hark to the e - choes, hear them play O - ver the hills and far a - way.

Merrily, merrily greet the morn,
Cheerily, cheerily sound the horn.
Hark to the echoes, hear them play
Over the hills and far away.

## 7. White Coral Bells

White co - ral bells u - pon a slen - der stock.

Li - lies of the val - ley deck our gar - den walk. O don't you wish that

you could hear them ring? That can hap - pen on - ly when the fai - ries sing.

White coral bells upon a slender stalk.
Lilies of the valley deck our garden walk.
O don't you wish that you could hear them ring?
That can happen only when the fairies sing.

## 8. Scotland's Burning

Scot - land's burn - ing! Scot - land's burn - ing! Look out! Look out!

Fi - re! Fi - re! Fi - re! Fi - re! Pour on wa - ter! Pour on wa - ter!

Scotland's burning! Scotland's burning!
Look out! Look out!
Fire! Fire! Fire! Fire!
Pour on water! Pour on water!

## 9. Fire's Burning

Fire's burn - ing, fire's burn - ing. Draw near - er, draw near - er. In the gloa - ming, in the gloa - ming. Come sing and be mer - ry.

Fire's burning, fire's burning.
Draw nearer, draw nearer.
In the gloaming, in the gloaming,
Come sing and be merry.

## 10. Hey Ho, Nobody Home

Hey, ho, no - bo - dy home. Meat nor drink nor mo - ney have I none, Yet will I be mer - ry, er - ry, er - ry, er - ry, er - ry.

Hey, ho, nobody home.
Meat nor drink nor money have I none,
Yet will I be merry.

## 11. To Ope Their Trunks

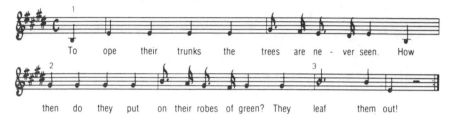

To ope their trunks the trees are never seen.
How then do they put on their robes of green?
They leaf them out!

## 12. Follow, Follow

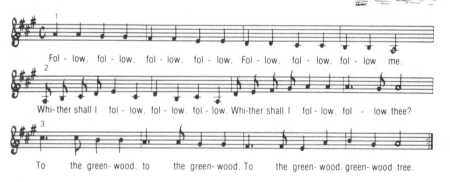

Follow, follow, follow, follow,
Follow, follow, follow me.
Whither shall I follow, follow, follow,
Whither shall I follow, follow thee?
To the greenwood, to the greenwood,
To the greenwood, greenwood tree.

### 13. Rheumatism, Rheumatism

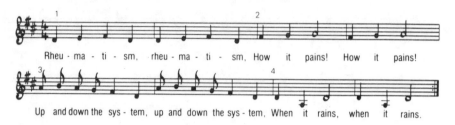

Rheumatism, rheumatism,
How it pains! How it pains!
Up and down the system, up and down the system,
When it rains, when it rains.


### 14. Turn Again, Whittington

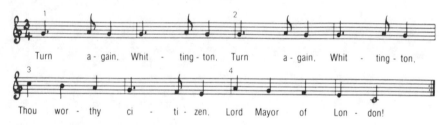

Turn again, Whittington,
Turn again, Whittington,
Thou worthy citizen,
Lord Mayor of London!

## 15. *Sweetly Sings the Donkey*

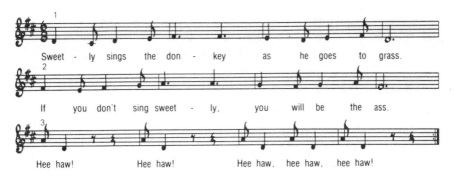

**A**

Sweetly sings the donkey as he goes to grass.
If you don't sing sweetly, you will be the ass.
Hee haw! Hee haw! Hee haw, hee haw, hee haw!

**B**

Sweetly sings the donkey as he goes to hay.
Someone must go with him or he'll run away.
Kee-I! Kee-O! Kee-I, Kee-O, Kee-Ay!

## 16. Grasshoppers Three

Grass-hop-pers three a - fid - dl - ing went. Hey, ho, ne - ver be still! They
paid no mo - ney to - ward their rent. But all day long with el - bow bent They
fid - dled a tune called Ril - la - by - ril - la - by, Fid - dled a tune called Ril - la - by - rill.

Grasshoppers three a-fiddling went,
Hey, ho, never be still!
They paid no money toward their rent,
But all day long with elbow bent
They fiddled a tune called Rillaby-rillaby,
Fiddled a tune called Rillaby-rill.

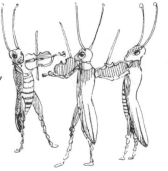

## 17. White Sand and Grey Sand

White sand and grey sand, Who'll buy my white sand? Who'll buy my grey sand?

White sand and grey sand,
Who'll buy my white sand?
Who'll buy my grey sand?

## 18  *My Aunt has a Lame Tame Crane*

My aunt has a lame tame crane.
My aunt has a crane that is lame.
Dear cousin Jane, let my aunt's lame tame crane
Feed and come home again.

## 19.  *My Paddle's Keen and Bright*

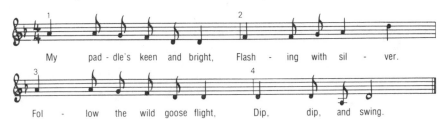

My paddle's keen and bright,
Flashing with silver.
Follow the wild goose flight,
Dip, dip, and swing.

Dip, dip, and swing her back,
Flashing with silver.
Swift as the wild goose flies,
Dip, dip, and swing.

## 20. *Man's Life*

Man's life's a vapour, full of woes.
He cuts a caper—down he goes.
Down he, down he, down he, down he, down he goes!

## 21. *All Things on Earth*

All things on earth shall fade under the sky.
Music alone shall live, music alone shall live,
Music alone shall live, and never die.

# Riddles in Rhyme

**22.**

Little Nancy Etticoat
In a white petticoat
And a red nose.
The longer she stands
The shorter she grows.
*(A candle)*

**23.**

Daffydowndilly's
Come up to town
In a yellow petticoat
And a green gown.
*(A daffodil)*

**24.**

Riddle me, riddle me, rote tote tote,
A wee red man with a wee red coat,
A stick in his hand, a stone in his throat:
Tell me this riddle and I'll give you a groat.
*(A cherry)*

**25.**

In spring I am gay
In handsome array.
In summer more clothing I wear.
When colder it grows,
I throw off my clothes,
And in winter quite naked appear.
*(A tree)*

**26.**

Old Lady Twitchett she had but one eye
And a great long tail that she let fly,
And every time that she went through a gap
She left a bit of her tail in the trap.
*(A needle)*

**27.**

I have a little sister,
I call her Pretty Peep.
She wades in the water
Deep, deep, deep.
She climbs on the mountains
High, high, high.
Poor little sister,
She has but one eye.
*(A star)*

**28.**

There was a thing just four weeks old
When Adam was no more.
Before that thing was five weeks old,
Old Adam was four score.
*(The moon)*

**29.**

In marble halls as white as milk,
Lined with a skin as soft as silk,
Within a fountain crystal clear
A golden apple doth appear.
There are no gates to this stronghold,
Yet thieves break in and steal the gold.
*(An egg)*

**30.**

A box without hinges, key or lid,
Yet golden treasure inside is hid.
*(An egg)*

**31.**

As white as milk, as soft as silk,
And hundreds close together;
They sail away on an autumn day
When windy is the weather.
*(Milkweed seeds)*

**32.**

I move without wings
Between silken strings.
I leave as you find
My substance behind.
*(A spider)*

**33.**

I have wings yet never fly;
I have sails yet never go.
I cannot keep still if I try,
Yet forever stand just so.
*(A windmill)*

**34.**

I tremble at all breaths of air
And yet the heaviest burdens bear.
*(Water)*

**35.**

What is round as an orange and deep as a cup,
Yet all the king's men can't pull it up?
*(A well)*

**36.**

Elizabeth, Lizzie, Betsy, and Bess
All went together to find a bird's nest.
They found a nest with five eggs in it;
They each took one and left four in it.
*(All names for the same girl)*

**37.**

Brothers and sisters have I none,
But that man's father was my father's son.
*(Man looking at his own picture)*

**38.**

Patch on patch without any stitches,
If you give me the answer I'll buy you some britches.
*(A cabbage)*

**39.**

Four stiff-standers,
Four dilly-danders,
Two lookers, two crookers,
And a long wiggle-waggle.
*(A cow)*

**40.**

What is small at the bottom and big at the top,
And the thing in the middle goes whipputy-whop?
(*Dash churn*)

**41.**

Around the rick, around the rick,
'Twas there I met my Uncle Dick.
I pulled off his head and drank his blood,
And left the body standing.
(*A bottle of wine*)

**42.**

What is round as a dishpan, deep as a tub,
And still the ocean cannot fill it up?
(*A sieve*)

**43.**

What's round like an apple,
Shaped like a pear,
With a slit in the middle
All covered with hair?
(*A peach*)

**44.**

Made long ago, yet made today,
Employed while others sleep,
What few would wish to give away,
And none would wish to keep.
(*A bed*)

**45.**

Round as an apple, hollow as a drum,
Lift its tail and its nose will run.
(*A hose pipe*)

**46.**

Round as an apple, flat as a chip,
Got two eyes and can't see a bit.
(*A button*)

**47.**

I have a wee horse with an iron throat.
As fast as he gallops, he swallows the rope.
(*A sewing machine*)

**48.**

Walk on the living, they don't even mumble.
Walk on the dead, they grumble and grumble.
(*Leaves*)

**49.**

What has a bed yet never sleeps,
And a mouth but never speaks?
(*A river*)

**50.**

What is it you can touch
And also you can feel?
It has neither size nor shape,
But just the same, it's real.
(*Air*)

**51.**

A hill full, a hole full,
You couldn't catch a bowl full.
*(Smoke)*

**52.**

Comes in at every window
And every door crack,
Runs around and round the house
But never leaves a track.
*(The wind)*

**53.**

Two hands without fingers,
Two feet without toes,
A round white face,
But never a nose.
It always stands still,
But it always goes.
*(A clock)*

**54.**

Thirty-two horses on a red hill.
Now they stamp, now they champ,
Now they stand still.
*(Teeth)*

**55.**

Flour of England,
Fruit of Spain,
Met together
In a shower of rain.

Put in a bag,
Tied up with a string.
If you tell me this riddle,
I'll give you a ring.
*(A plum pudding)*

**56.**

My first is a circle,
My second a cross.
If you meet with my whole,
Look out for a toss.
*(OX)*

**57.**

What's in the mill and not in the hopper?
What's in the dam and not in water?
What's in the mountain and not in the plain?
What's in Jamaica and not in Spain?
*(M)*

**58.**

Three-quarters of a cross, a circle complete,
Two semi-circles and a perpendicular meet,
An equilateral triangle standing on two feet,
Two semi-circles, and a circle complete.
*(TOBACCO)*

**59.**

Two N's, two O's, an L, and a D.
Put them together and spell them to me.
*(London)*

**60.**

On yonder hill there is a mill.
Around that mill there is a walk.
Under that walk there is a key.
What is the name of that mill?
*(Milwaukee)*

**61.**

Down on a yellow mat I saw a lump of fat,
Four and twenty carpenters working at that,
Some with yellow bonnets, some with black hats.
If you don't tell me this riddle, I'll give you three slaps.
*(A beehive)*

**62.**

In a garden was laid a pretty fair maid,
As fair as the light of the morn.
The first day of her life she was made a wife,
And she died before she was born.
*(Eve)*

**63.**

My first is in warlock and wizard and white,
My second's in shiver and also in fright,
My third will appear in broomstick and cat,
My fourth is in magic, though never in mat,
My fifth you will find in high and in hill,
My whole is a person who practises ill.
*(A witch)*

## 64. King Henry Has Set Me Free

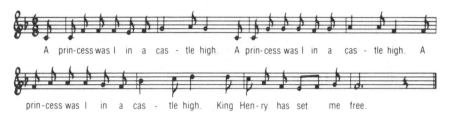

A prin-cess was I in a cas - tle high. A prin-cess was I in a cas - tle high. A

prin-cess was I in a cas - tle high. King Hen-ry has set me free.

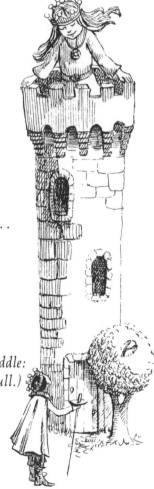

A princess was I in a castle high.
A princess was I in a castle high.
A princess was I in a castle high.
  King Henry has set me free.

As I walked out and in again,
As I walked out and in again,
As I walked out and in again,
  King Henry has set me free.

'Twas from the dead the living came . . .

Oh, six there were, and seven there'll be . . .

A napkin hung on a silver pin . . .

All for to wipe my tears of sin . . .

Now I'm Queen Esther in a castle high . . .

*(To release the princess, someone has to guess the riddle:
that there were six birds and an egg in a horse's skull.)*

# Animal Fair

## 65. The Animal Fair

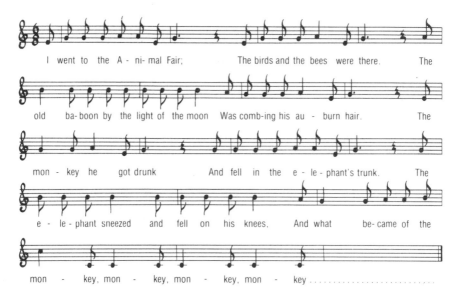

I went to the A - ni- mal Fair; The birds and the bees were there. The
old ba-boon by the light of the moon Was comb-ing his au - burn hair. The
mon - key he got drunk And fell in the e - le - phant's trunk. The
e - le - phant sneezed and fell on his knees, And what be- came of the
mon - key, mon - key, mon - key, mon - key

I went to the Animal Fair;
The birds and the bees were there.
The old baboon by the light of the moon
Was combing his auburn hair.
The monkey he got drunk
And fell in the elephant's trunk.
The elephant sneezed and fell on his knees,
And what became of the monkey, monkey, monkey ...

*(Continue until tired.)*

## 66. *The Tune the Old Cow Died On*

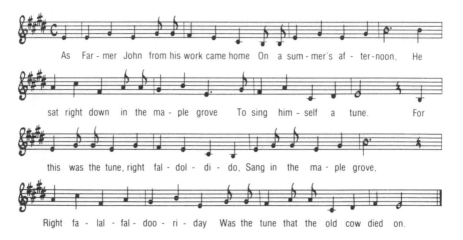

As Far-mer John from his work came home On a sum-mer's af-ter-noon. He
sat right down in the ma-ple grove To sing him-self a tune. For
this was the tune, right fal-dol-di-do, Sang in the ma-ple grove,
Right fa-lal-fal-doo-ri-day Was the tune that the old cow died on.

As Farmer John from his work came home
On a summer's afternoon,
He sat right down in the maple grove
To sing himself a tune.

REFRAIN:

For this was the tune, right fal-dol-di-do,
Sang in the maple grove,
Right fa-lal fal-doo-ri-day
Was the tune that the old cow died on.

The cows all got around him
And circled in a ring,
For they never heard old Farmer John
Attempt before to sing.

The oldest cow in the farmer's flock
Tried hard to sing that song,
But she could not reach the melody
Though her voice was loud and strong.

34

The farmer laughed till the tears ran down
His cheeks like cherries red,
And the cow she tried to sing that song
Until she dropped down dead.

Now Farmer John had an inquest held
To see what killed his cow.
The jury sat and the verdict brought
Which I mean to tell you now.

They said that the cow might be living yet
To chew her cud with glee
If Farmer John hadn't sung that song
Beneath the maple tree.

## 67.   *The Horse Named Napoleon*

TUNE: REUBEN AND RACHEL

I once had a horse and his name was Napoleon,
Named on account of his bony parts.
Bought him from an old Post Indian
Known to everyone in these parts.

He was so thin you could see right through him,
Hair was as soft as the finest silk.
Hitched him to an old milk wagon,
Taught him to stop when I yelled "Milk!"

Along came a dude in the finest livery,
Said to me, "Son, would you run a race?"
Sure as a sinner I was coming in a winner
When the dude yelled "Milk!" and I lost that race.

## 68. The Derby Ram

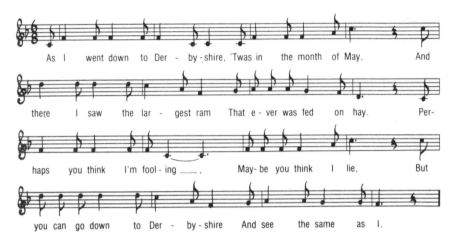

As I went down to Derbyshire, 'Twas in the month of May, And there I saw the lar - gest ram That e - ver was fed on hay. Per-haps you think I'm fool - ing ___, May-be you think I lie, But you can go down to Der - by - shire And see the same as I.

As I went down to Derbyshire,
'Twas in the month of May,
And there I saw the largest ram
That ever was fed on hay.

REFRAIN:

Perhaps you think I'm fooling,
Maybe you think I lie,
But you can go down to Derbyshire
And see the same as I.

The wool upon his back, sir,
It grew up to the sky.
The eagles built their nests in it–
I could hear the young ones cry.

The horns upon that ram, sir,
They grew up to the moon.
A man went up in April
And he never came down till June.

This ram he had four feet, sir,
And on them he did stand,
And every foot he had, sir,
Would cover an acre of land.

Now every tooth he had, sir,
Was hollow as a horn.
They took one out and measured it–
It held a barrel of corn.

Now the man that killed this ram, sir,
Was up to his knees in blood.
The one that held the basin
Was washed away in the flood.

**69.** *The Wee Lambie*

There was a wee lambie fell over a rock,
And when it fell over its leg it was broke,
And all that the poor little lambie could do
Was to lie and cry out, "Billaloo, billaloo."

## 70. *The Goat*

There was a man (there was a man), now please take note (now please take note). There was a man (there was a man) who had a goat (who had a goat). He loved that goat (he loved that goat), in-deed he did (in-deed he did). He loved that goat (he loved that goat) just like a kid. (just like a kid).

There was a man (there was a man), now please take note
    (now please take note),
There was a man (there was a man) who had a goat
    (who had a goat).
He loved that goat (he loved that goat), indeed he did
    (indeed he did),
He loved that goat (he loved that goat) just like a kid.

One day that goat felt frisk and fine,
Ate three red shirts from off the line.
He hit that goat an awful whack
And tied it to the railroad track.

And when the train hove into sight
The goat grew pale and green with fright,
Then heaved a sigh as if in pain,
Coughed up those shirts and flagged the train.

## 71. *Mary Had a William Goat*

Ma - ry had a Wil - liam goat, Wil - liam goat, Wil - liam goat,

Ma - ry had a Wil - liam goat, his sto-mach was lined with zinc.

Mary had a William goat, William goat, William goat,
Mary had a William goat, his stomach was lined with zinc.

One day he ate an oyster can, oyster can, oyster can,
One day he ate an oyster can, and a kitchen sink.

The can was filled with dynamite, dynamite, dynamite,
The can was filled with dynamite, which Billy thought
    was cheese.

He rubbed against poor Mary's side, Mary's side, Mary's
    side,
He rubbed against poor Mary's side the awful pain to ease.

A sudden flash of goat and girl, goat and girl, goat and girl,
A sudden flash of goat and girl, and little else to tell.

Mary's soul to heaven went, heaven went, heaven went,
Mary's soul to heaven went, and Billy's went to———.

Hoop dee doodle doodle doo, doodle doo, doodle doo,
Hoop dee doodle doodle doo, hoop dee doodle doo.

## 72.  *The Three Little Pigs*

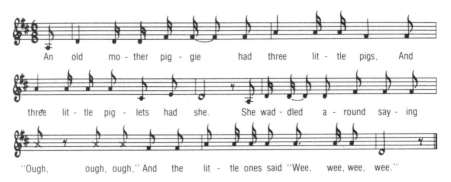

An old mother piggie had three little pigs,
And three little piglets had she.
She waddled around saying "Ough, ough, ough,"
And the little ones said "Wee, wee, wee, wee."

Now one day one of these three little pigs
To his two brothers said he,
"From now on let's always say 'Ough, ough, ough.'
It's so childish to say 'Wee, wee, wee, wee.'"

Now these three piggies grew skinny and thin,
And thin they might very well be,
Because they just couldn't say "Ough, ough, ough,"
And they wouldn't say "Wee, wee, wee, wee."

At last these three piggies they lay down and died,
A very sad sight to see,
Because they just couldn't say "Ough, ough, ough,"
And they wouldn't say "Wee, wee, wee, wee."

A moral there is to this sad little tale,
A moral that's plain to see:
You never should try to say "Ough, ough, ough,"
When you only can say "Wee, wee, wee, wee."

## 73.  *The Fox and the Goose*

A fox roved out one very dark night,
He prayed that the moon would give good light,
For he had a long way to travel that night
Before he'd a-reach his den, den,
Before he'd a-reach his den.

Then he travelled and he travelled till he came to a yard,
The ducks and geese they all lay abroad.
"The best one of you must grace my beard
Before I go over the town, town,
Before I go over the town."

Then he grabbed the grey goose up by the neck,
And up he slung her onto his back
As if she were a gunny sack,
And the blood came trinkling down, down,
And the blood came trinkling down.

Then old Mother Quickenquacker jumped out of bed;
She opened the window and poked out her head:
"Arise, arise, the grey goose is dead,
And the fox has gone over the town, town,
And the fox has gone over the town."

Then Johnny arose and went to the hill;
He blew his bugle loud and shrill.
"Blow on," said the fox, "till you've had your fill,
But I'm glad I got out of your town, town,
But I'm glad I got out of your town."

The fox travelled on till he came to a plain;
He rested his burden to ease his pain,
But it wasn't very long 'fore he took her up again,
And then he heard the cry of the hounds, hounds,
And then he heard the cry of the hounds.

The fox travelled on till he came to his den
Where he had young ones nine or ten.
"Welcome home, daddy fox, you must go back again,
For we think it's a very lucky town, town,
For we think it's a very lucky town."

Oh, the fox and his wife they made such a strife,
They said they never ate a better bird in their life,
So they tore up the grey goose without a knife,
And the young ones nibbled at the bones, bones,
And the young ones nibbled at the bones.

## 74. The Fox and the Grapes

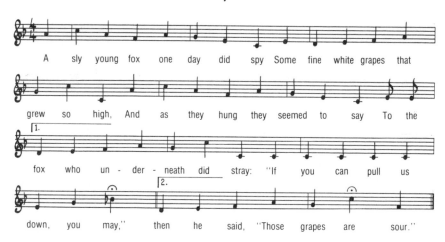

A sly young fox one day did spy Some fine white grapes that
grew so high, And as they hung they seemed to say To the
fox who un - der - neath did stray: "If you can pull us
down, you may," then he said, "Those grapes are sour."

A sly young fox one day did spy
Some fine white grapes that grew so high,
And as they hung they seemed to say
To the fox who underneath did stray:
"If you can pull us down, you may."

Oh, the fox nearly his patience lost,
With all his expectations crossed.
He licked his lips for near an hour
But found the grapes beyond his power,
And then he said, "Those grapes are sour."

## 75. The Presbyterian Cat

TUNE: AULD LANG SYNE

There was a Presbyterian cat
Went searching for her prey
And foond a moose within the hoose
Upon the Sawbath day.

43

The people all were horrified
And they were grieved sair,
And straightway led that wicked cat
Before the ministaire.

The ministaire was horrified
And unto her did say:
"Oh naughty cat, to catch a moose
Upon the Sawbath day.

"The Sawbath's been, fra days of yore,
An in-sti-tu-ti-on."
So they straightway led that wicked cat
To ex-e-cu-ti-on.

(THE MORAL)

The higher up the plum tree grows,
The sweeter grow the plums;
The more the cobbler plies his trade,
The broader grow his thumbs.

## 76. The Frog in the Well

There was a frog lived in a well, lay, lin - ky lay! There
was a frog lived in a well, How he got out I can - not tell.
Lay, link! Lay, link! Lin - ky - lo lal - ly - lo lay!

There was a frog lived in a well, lay, linky-lay!
There was a frog lived in a well,
How he got out I cannot tell.
Lay, link! Lay, link! Linky-lo lally-lo lay!

He rode till he came to Miss Mousie's door, lay, linky-lay!
He rode till he came to Miss Mousie's door
And hollered as loud as he could roar.
Lay, link! Lay, link! Linky-lo lally-lo lay!

"Pray, Mistress Mouse, are you within?" Lay, linky-lay!
"Pray, Mistress Mouse, are you within?"
"Oh, yes, kind sir, you can hear me spin."
Lay, link! Lay, link! Linky-lo lally-lo lay!

He took Miss Mouse upon his knee . . .
And said, "Little mouse, will you marry me?" . . .

"Oh, no, kind sir, I can't do that . . .
Without consent of Mr. Rat." . . .

Oh, Mr. Rat came riding home . . .
Says, "Who's been here since I've been gone?" . . .

"A fine young gentleman of high degree . . .
He wants to know if he can marry me." . . .

Oh, Mr. Rat gave his consent . . .
And off to the wedding supper they went . . .

The first to come was Mr. Bee . . .
He stung the bride upon the knee . . .

The next to come was Mr. Snake . . .
He rolled himself round the wedding cake . . .

The next to come was Mrs. Bug . . .
She brought the bride a brand new rug . . .

The old black cat jumped over the wall . . .
And ate the rat, the mouse, and all . . .

If you want any more you can sing it yourself . . .
The book lies on the pantry shelf . . .

## 77. Mr. Rat and Miss Mouse

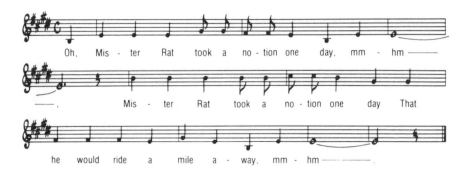

Oh, Mis - ter Rat took a no - tion one day, mm - hm —— Mis - ter Rat took a no - tion one day That he would ride a mile a - way. mm - hm ——.

Oh, Mr. Rat took a notion one day, mmhm,
Oh, Mr. Rat took a notion one day
That he would ride a mile away, mmhm, mmhm.

He rode right down to Miss Mouse's home, mmhm,
He rode right down to Miss Mouse's home,
He said, "Miss Mouse, are you all alone?" Mmhm, mmhm.

He took Miss Mouse upon his knee . . .
And he said, "Miss Mouse, will you marry me?" . . .

Said little Miss Mouse, "I can't say that . . .
You'll have to ask my Uncle Rat." . . .

Uncle Rat gave his consent ...
That they should marry and be content ...

Where will the wedding supper be? ...
Way down under the cherry tree ...

The first to come was a little brown chick ...
Who ate so much that he made himself sick ...

Had to call for Dr. Fly ...
For fear the little brown chick would die ...

The next to come was a big brown bear ...
Who sat himself in the rocking chair ...

The next to come was a long green snake ...
Who curled his tail round the wedding cake ...

The wedding cake sits on the shelf ...
If you want any more you can help yourself ...

## 78. *The Little Kitty*

TUNE: COMING THROUGH THE RYE

Once there was a little kitty
Whiter than the snow.
In the barn she used to play
    Long time ago.

In the barn a little mousie
Running to and fro
For she heard the kitty coming
    Long time ago.

Two black eyes has little kitty,
Black as any sloe,
And they spied the little mousie
    Long time ago.

Four soft paws has little kitty
As swift as any doe,
And they caught the little mousie
    Long time ago.

Nine front teeth has little kitty
All in a row,
And they bit the little mousie
    Long time ago.

When the teeth bit little mousie
Sore she cried "Oh!"
But she got away from kitty
    Long time ago.

## 79.   *The Crocodile*

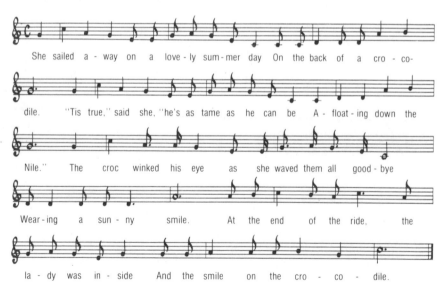

She sailed a - way on a love - ly sum - mer day On the back of a cro - co-
dile. "Tis true," said she, "he's as tame as he can be A - float - ing down the
Nile." The croc winked his eye as she waved them all good - bye
Wear - ing a sun - ny smile. At the end of the ride, the
la - dy was in - side And the smile on the cro - co - dile.

She sailed away on a lovely summer day
On the back of a crocodile.
"'Tis true," said she, "he's as tame as he can be
A-floating down the Nile."
The croc winked his eye as she waved them all good-bye
Wearing a sunny smile.
At the end of the ride, the lady was inside
And the smile on the crocodile.

**80.** *The Whale*

TUNE: DIXIE

In Puget Sound there lives a whale:
She eats peanuts by the pail,
By the pillbox, by the carload,
By the cargo and the schooner.

Oh, her name's Sarah and she's all right,
But she eats everything in sight–
From babies to nursemaids,
To chocolate ice-cream sodas.

Oh, she's all right, but when she smiles
You can see her teeth for miles and miles,
And her tonsils, and her adenoids,
And things too fierce to mention.

Oh, what can you do with a whale like that?
What can you do if she sits on your hat,
Or your toothbrush, or your mother-in-law,
Or anything else that's helpless?

## 81. *The Roaring Crocodile*

Good friends and all, on you I call, come listen unto me
While I relate my hardships great and the dangers of the sea.
Shipwrecked I was in the last storm, and I was cast on shore,
I took a trip to Alaska all that country to explore.

I travelled on four months or more, when right broadside
    the ocean
I saw something seemed to move like all the world in motion.
I quickly then drew up to it; it was a crocodile.
From the end of his nose to the tip of his tail was
    nineteen hundred miles.

This crocodile as you may see was none of the common race,
For I had to climb a very high tree before I could see his face.
The wind it blew a bitter gale a-coming from the south,
And there by chance I lost my grip, fell into the crocodile's
    mouth.

He quickly closed his jaws on me, he thought he'd gained
    a victim,
But I slipped down his throat you see, and that's the way
    I tricked him.

I travelled on four months or more until I reached his belly,
And there was scores of stuff and stores, plenty of rum
    and jelly.

And for to drive small cares away, I'm sure I wasn't stinted
For I lived there for seven years, was very well contented.
This crocodile was growing old; at length one day he died.
He was seven years in getting cold, he was so long and wide.

His skin you see was nine miles thick, or somewheres
    there about,
For it took me seven years or more a-cutting a hole to get out.
And if you think this is not true, whenever you cross the isle
If you look well, you'll see the shell of the roaring crocodile.

## 82. *Go Tell Aunt Abbie*

Go tell Aunt Ab - bie. Go tell Aunt Ab - bie.

Go tell Aunt Ab - bie Her old grey goose is dead.

Go tell Aunt Abbie,
Go tell Aunt Abbie,
Go tell Aunt Abbie
Her old grey goose is dead.

The one she was saving,
The one she was saving,
The one she was saving
To make a feather bed.

She died in the mill pond,
She died in the mill pond,

51

She died in the mill pond
Standing on her head.

The barnyard is weeping,
The barnyard is weeping,
The barnyard is weeping
Wanting to be fed.

The boys they are freezing,
The boys they are freezing,
The boys they are freezing
Because they have no bed.

We'll have to kill old gander,
We'll have to kill old gander,
We'll have to kill old gander
To make the boys a bed.

### 83. *Mistress Bond*

Oh what shall we have for dinner, Mistress Bond? There's
geese in the lar - der and ducks in the pond, Cry- ing, "Dil- ly, dil - ly, dil - ly dil - ly,
come to be killed, For you must be stuffed and our cus - tom -ers filled."

Oh, what shall we have for dinner, Mistress Bond?
There's geese in the larder and ducks in the pond,
Crying, "Dilly, dilly, dilly, dilly, come to be killed,
For you must be stuffed and our customers filled."

"John Ostler, go fetch me a duckling or two.
John Ostler, go fetch me a duckling or two.
Cry, 'Dilly, dilly, dilly, dilly, come to be killed,
For you must be stuffed and our customers filled.'"

"I have been to the ducks that are swimming in the pond,
And they refuse to come to be killed, Mistress Bond.
I said, 'Come, little waggle-tails, come to be killed,
For you must be stuffed and our customers filled.'"

Well, Mistress Bond she went down to the pond in a rage,
Her apron full of onions, her pockets full of sage.
She cried, "Dilly, dilly, dilly, dilly, come to be killed,
For you must be stuffed and our customers filled."

Said the ducklings politely, "No, thank you, Mistress Bond.
We will not come to dinner; we like our little pond.
We are wise little ducklings; we won't be killed.
No, we'll not be stuffed, nor your customers filled."

## 84. *Three Crows*

There were three crows sat on a tree. Sing Bil-ly Mc-Gee Mc-Gaw. There
were three crows sat on a tree. Sing Bil-ly Mc-Gee Mc-Gaw. There
were three crows sat on a tree And they were black as crows could be. And they
all flapped their wings and cried: "Caw, Caw, Caw, Caw," Bil-ly Mc-Gee Mc-
Gaw." And they all flapped their wings and cried: "Bil-ly Mc-Gee Mc-Gaw."

There were three crows sat on a tree,
     Sing Billy McGee McGaw,
There were three crows sat on a tree,
     Sing Billy McGee McGaw,
There were three crows sat on a tree
And they were black as crows could be.


REFRAIN:

And they all flapped their wings and cried:
"Caw, Caw, Caw, Caw, Billy McGee McGaw."
And they all flapped their wings and cried:
"Billy McGee McGaw."

Said one old crow unto his mate,
     Sing Billy McGee McGaw,
Said one old crow unto his mate,
     Sing Billy McGee McGaw,

Said one old crow unto his mate:
"What shall we have for grub to eat?"

"There lies a horse on yonder plain,
    Sing Billy McGee McGaw,
There lies a horse on yonder plain,
    Sing Billy McGee McGaw,
There lies a horse on yonder plain,
You peck his bones, I'll eat his brain."

## 85. *Three Craws*

Three craws sat u-pon a wa', Sat u-pon a wa', sat u-pon a wa'. Three craws sat u-pon a wa', So ear-ly in the morn-ing.

Three craws sat upon a wa',
Sat upon a wa', sat upon a wa'.
Three craws sat upon a wa',
So early in the morning.

REFRAIN:

Ha, ha, ha ha ha ha ha,
Ha ha ha ha ha, ha ha ha ha ha,
Ha, ha, ha ha ha ha ha,
So early in the morning.

First craw he flew off the wa',
He flew off the wa', he flew off the wa'.
First craw he flew off the wa',
So early in the morning.

Second craw he fell off the wa',
He fell off the wa', he fell off the wa'.
Second craw he fell off the wa',
So early in the morning.

Third craw he wasna there at a',
Wasna there at a', wasna there at a'.
Third craw he wasna there at a',
So early in the morning.

## 86.  *Who Killed Cock Robin?*

Who killed Cock Robin?
"I," said the Sparrow,
"With my bow and arrow,
I killed Cock Robin."

REFRAIN:

Then the birds of the air
Fell a-sighing and a-sobbing
When they heard of the death
Of poor Cock Robin,

When they heard of the death
Of poor Cock Robin.

Who saw him die?
"I," said the Fly,
"With my little eye,
I saw him die."

Who caught his blood?
"I," said the Fish,
"With my little dish,
I caught his blood."

Who'll dig his grave?
"I," said the Owl,
"With my paddock and trowel,
I'll dig his grave."

Who'll be chief mourner?
"I," said the Rook,
"Because I can croak,
I'll be chief mourner."

### 87. The Birdies' Ball

Spring once said to the night-in-gale: "I mean to give you
birds a ball. Pray, Ma'am, you ask the bir-dies all, The
birds and the bir-dies great and small." Tra - la - la - la - la,
tra - la - la - la - la, Tra-la-la-la-la-la-la-la-la-la - la - la.

Spring once said to the nightingale:
"I mean to give you birds a ball.
Pray, ma'am, you ask the birdies all,
The birds and the birdies, great and small."

REFRAIN:

Tra-la-la-la-la, tra-la-la-la-la,
Tra-la-la-la-la-la-la.

Soon they came from bush and tree,
Singing sweet their songs of glee.
Each one fresh from its cosy nest
And each one dressed in its Sunday best.

The wren and the cuckoo danced for life;
The raven waltzed with the yellow bird's wife.
The awkward owl and the bashful jay
Wished each other a very good day.

58

The woodpecker came from his hole in the tree;
He brought his bill for the company,
For cherries ripe, for berries red:
'Twas a very long bill, so the birdies said.

They danced all day till the sun was low,
Till the mother birds prepared to go,
When one and all, both great and small,
Flew home to their nests from the birdies' ball.

## 88. *The Swapping Song*

When I was a young man I lived by myself
On the bread and cheese that was laid upon the shelf.

REFRAIN:

Come a wing wang waddle, come a jack straw straddle,
Come the don fair faddle, come a long way home.

The rats and the mice they led me such a life
I had to go to London to get myself a wife.

The streets were so wide, the bridges were so narrow,
I had to bring her home in an old wheelbarrow.

The wheelbarrow broke and we all had a fall.
Down came wheelbarrow, wife, and all.

I sold my wife and got me a horse,
And then I rode from course to course.

I sold my horse and bought me a mare,
And then I rode from fair to fair.

I swapped my mare and got me a cow,
And on that deal I just learned how.

I swapped my cow and got me a calf,
And on that deal I just got half.

I swapped my calf and got me a sheep,
And there I rode till I fell asleep.

I swapped my sheep and got me a hen.
Oh, what a pretty thing I had then!

# Tongue Twisters

**89.**

Betty Botter bought some butter,
And she said, "This butter's bitter.
If I put it in my batter
It will make my batter bitter,
But a bit of better butter
Would but make my batter better."
So 'twas better Betty Botter
Bought a bit of better butter.

**90.**

Peter Piper picked a peck of pickled peppers.
A peck of pickled peppers Peter Piper picked.
If Peter Piper picked a peck of pickled peppers,
Where is the peck of pickled peppers Peter Piper picked?

**91.**

How much wood would a woodchuck chuck
If a woodchuck could chuck wood?
A woodchuck would chuck all the wood he could chuck
If a woodchuck could chuck wood.

**92.**

She sells sea shells on the seashore.
The shells she sells are sea shells I'm sure,
For if she sells sea shells on the seashore,
Then I'm sure she sells seashore shells.

**93.**

Swan swam over the sea.
Swim, swan, swim.
Swan swam back again.
Well swum, swan!

**94.**

If a shipshape ship shop stocks
Six shipshape shop-soiled ships,
How many shipshape shop-soiled ships
Would six shipshape ship shops stock?

**95.**

Bill had a billboard. Bill also had a board bill.
The board bill bored Bill,
So Bill sold his billboard to pay his board bill.
The board bill no longer bored Bill.

**96.**

Knott was not in.
Knott was out knotting knots in netting.
Knott was out,
But lots of knots were in Knott's netting.

**97.**

Three grey geese in a green field grazing.
Grey were the geese, and green was the grazing.

**98.**

Shiny Susy sitting on a shining wall.
The more she sits, she shines.
The more she shines, she sits.

**99.**

Moses supposes his toeses are roses,
But Moses supposes erroneously,
For nobody's toeses are posies of roses
As Moses supposes his toeses to be.

**100.**
Seventy-six sick soldiers saw
Six slimy snakes slither southwards.

**101.**

Theophilus Thistle, the thistle-sifter, sifted some thistles.
If Theophilus Thistle, the thistle-sifter, sifted some thistles,
Where are the thistles that Theophilus Thistle, the thistle-
     sifter, sifted?

**102.**

Which switch is the switch, miss, for Ipswich?
It is the Ipswich switch which I desire.
Which switch switches my switch for Ipswich?
You switched my switch on the wrong wire.
You switched me on Norwich, not Ipswich,
And now to prevent further hitch
If you'll tell me which is Norwich, which Ipswich,
Then we'll know which switch is which.

**103.**

A skunk sat on a stump.
The stump thought the skunk stunk,
And the skunk thought the stump stunk.

**104.**

Big fat hen,
Couple of ducks,
Three brown bear,
Four running hare,
Five fat fantastic females,
Six sexy Siamese sailors sailing the seven seas,
Eight enormous elephants eating elongated eggplant,
Nine nifty nellies knitting knickers nightly,
Ten tractor-trailers trucking tomatoes from Toronto to
     Tonawanda today, tonight, and tomorrow.

**105.**

One old ox opening oysters.
Two toads, totally tired, trying to trot to Tilbury.
Three thick, thumping tigers, tickling trout.
Four fat friars fanning fainting fleas.
Five fanciful females fleeing for fashions from France.
Six silly sailors singing saucy songs.
Seven Severn salmon seeking sorrowful seclusion.
Eight elegant elephants elevating eager eyebrows.
Nine nimble noblemen nibbling nonpareil.
Ten twittering tomtits twittering atop tall trees.

# Endless Songs

# Circular Songs

## 106.  *Michael Finnigin*

There was an old man named Michael Finnigin.
He grew whiskers on his chin-i-gin.
The wind came up and blew them in ag'in.
Poor old Michael Finnigin. Begin ag'in.

## 107.  *John Jacob Jingleheimer Jones*

John Jacob Jingleheimer Jones–
That's my name, too.
Whenever I go out, the people always shout:
"JOHN JACOB JINGLEHEIMER JONES!" tra-la-la-la!
*(Repeat until tired.)*

**108.** *Sandy's Mill*

Sandy lent the man the mill,
And the man got the loan of Sandy's mill.
Said the man to Sandy, "Will you lend me your mill?"
"I'll lend you the mill," said Sandy.
Sandy lent the man the mill . . .
*(Repeat until tired.)*

**109.** *The Ragman and the Bagman*

A ragman and a bagman came to a farmer's barn.
Said the ragman to the bagman, "I'll do ye nae harm."
There are forty verses to my song,
And this is the first one just gone along.

A ragman and a bagman came to a farmer's barn.
Said the ragman to the bagman, "I'll do ye nae harm."

There are forty verses to my song,
And this is the second one just gone along ...
*(Continue up to forty, or until tired.)*


## 110.  *My Father Gave Me*

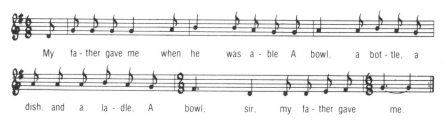

My fa-ther gave me when he was a-ble A bowl, a bot-tle, a
dish, and a la-dle. A bowl, sir, my fa-ther gave me.

My father gave me when he was able
A bowl, a bottle, a dish, and a ladle,
A bowl, sir, my father gave me.

My father gave me when he was able
A bowl, a bottle, a dish, and a ladle,
Two bowls, two bottles, two dishes, two ladles,
A bowl, sir, my father gave me.

My father gave me when he was able.
A bowl, a bottle, a dish, and a ladle,
Three bowls, three bottles, three dishes, three ladles,
A bowl, sir, my father gave me.
*(Continue up to twelve.)*

## 111. *She'll Be Comin' Round the Mountain*

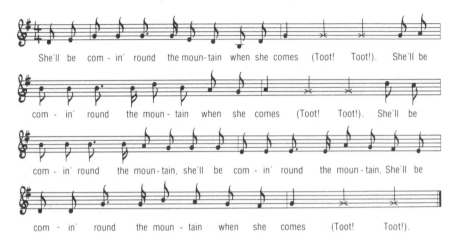

She'll be com-in' round the moun-tain when she comes (Toot! Toot!). She'll be

com - in' round the moun - tain when she comes (Toot! Toot!). She'll be

com - in' round the moun-tain, she'll be com - in' round the moun - tain, She'll be

com - in' round the moun - tain when she comes (Toot! Toot!).

She'll be comin' round the mountain when she comes
    (Toot! Toot!).
She'll be comin' round the mountain when she comes
    (Toot! Toot!).
She'll be comin' round the mountain, she'll be comin'
    round the mountain,
She'll be comin' round the mountain when she comes
    (Toot! Toot!).

She'll be driving six white horses when she comes
    (Whoa! Back!).
She'll be driving six white horses when she comes
    (Whoa! Back!).
She'll be driving six white horses, she'll be driving six
    white horses,
She'll be driving six white horses when she comes
    (Whoa! Back! Toot! Toot!).

She'll be wearing old red flannels when she comes
    (Scratch! Scratch!) ...

She'll be shooting off the pistols when she comes
(Bang! Bang!) . . .

Oh, we'll all go out to meet her when she comes
(Hi, Babe!) . . .

Oh, we'll kill the old red rooster when she comes
(Chop! Chop!) . . .

Oh, we'll all have chicken and dumplings when she comes
(Yum! Yum!) . . .

Oh, she'll have to sleep with Grandma when she comes
(Move over!) . . .

We'll be singing Hallelujah when she comes (Hallelujah!)
We'll be singing Hallelujah when she comes (Hallelujah!)
We'll be singing Hallelujah, we'll be singing Hallelujah,
We'll be singing Hallelujah when she comes
(Hallelujah! Move over! Yum! Yum! Chop! Chop!
Hi, Babe! Bang! Bang! Scratch! Scratch! Whoa! Back!
Toot! Toot!).

## 112. *Hole in the Ground*

There was a hole (there was a hole). Pret-tiest lit - tle

hole (pret-tiest lit - tle hole) That you e-ver did see (that you e-ver did see)

Hole in the ground And the green grass grew all a-

round, all a - round, And the green grass grew all a - round.

FIRST REFRAIN:

There was a hole (there was a hole),
Prettiest little hole (prettiest little hole)
That you ever did see (that you ever did see).

Hole in the ground
And the green grass grew all around, all around,
And the green grass grew all around.

Now in that hole (now in that hole)
There was a root (there was a root),
Prettiest little root (prettiest little root)
That you ever did see (that you ever did see).

SECOND REFRAIN:

Root in the hole and the hole in the ground
And the green grass grew all around, all around,
And the green grass grew all around.

Now on that root there was a tree ...

Now on that tree there was a branch ...

Now on that branch there was a nest ...

Now in that nest there was an egg ...

Now in that egg there was a bird ...

Now on that bird there was a wing ...

Now on that wing there was a feather ...

Now on that feather there was a bug ...

Now on that bug there was an eye ...

Now on that eye there was an eyelash ...

Now on that eyelash there was a hair ...

Now on that hair there was a speck ...

Now on that speck there was a germ ...

LAST REFRAIN:

Germ on the speck, speck on the hair, hair on the eyelash,
    eyelash on the eye, eye on the bug, bug on the feather,
    feather on the wing, wing on the bird, bird in the egg,
    egg in the nest, nest on the branch, branch on the tree,
    tree on the root, root in the ground,
And the green grass grew all around, all around,
And the green grass grew all around.

### 113. *The Wild Man of Borneo*

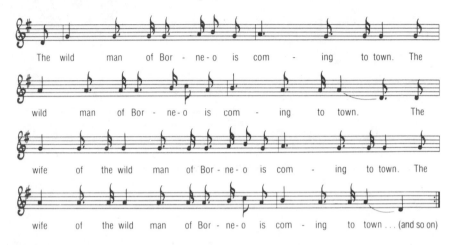

The wild man of Bor - ne - o is com - ing to town. The
wild man of Bor - ne - o is com - ing to town. The
wife of the wild man of Bor - ne - o is com - ing to town. The
wife of the wild man of Bor - ne - o is com - ing to town . . . (and so on)

The wild man of Borneo is coming to town.
The wild man of Borneo is coming to town.

The wife of the wild man of Borneo is coming to town.
The wife of the wild man of Borneo is coming to town.

The child of the wife of the wild man of Borneo is coming
to town. . .

The dog of the child of the wife of the wild man of Borneo . . .

The tail of the dog of the child of the wife of the wild man
of Borneo . . .

The hair on the tail of the dog of the child of the wife of
the wild man of Borneo . . .

The flea on the hair of the tail of the dog of the child of the
wife of the wild man of Borneo . . .

The speck on the flea on the hair of the tail of the dog of
the child of the wife of the wild man of Borneo . . .

## 114.  *The Mallard*

Oh, I have eaten him. What did I eat?
I ate the head of the mallard.
Head head and two two's and two nonnicks I know,
I have been to the Finnegan's ball,
And good meat was the mallard.

Oh, I have eaten him. What did I eat?
I ate the neck of the mallard.
Neck neck and head head and two two's and two nonnicks
    I know,
I have been to the Finnegan's ball,
And good meat was the mallard.

Oh, I have eaten him. What did I eat?
I ate the back of the mallard.
Back back and neck neck and head head and two two's and
    two nonnicks I know,
I have been to the Finnegan's ball,
And good meat was the mallard.

*(Continue for wing, side, breast, tail, leg, and toe.)*

## 115. Old King Twine

Oh, it's old King Twine and he called for his wine. And he called for his drum - mers three. And if e - ver a drum - mer could drum well. For a ve - ry fine drum had he. "Oh, rub - a - dub - a - dum," said the drum - mer. There's ne'er a band in old Scot - land Could play such a tune as this.

Oh, it's old King Twine and he called for his wine,
And he called for his drummers three,
And if ever a drummer could drum well,
For a very fine drum had he.
    "Oh, rub-a-dub-a-dum," said the drummer.
There's ne'er a band in old Scotland
Could play such a tune as this.

Oh, it's old King Twine and he called for his wine,
And he called for his fiddlers three,
And if ever a fiddler could fiddle well,
For a very fine fiddle had he.
    "Oh, yank-yanky-doodle," said the fiddler,
    "Rub-a-dub-a-dum," said the drummer.
There's ne'er a band in old Scotland
Could play such a tune as this.

Oh, it's old King Twine and he called for his wine
And he called for his fifers three,
And if ever a fifer could fife well,
For a very fine fife had he.
   "Oh, toodle-doodle-oo," said the fifer,
   "Yank-yanky-doodle," said the fiddler,
   "Rub-a-dub-a-dum," said the drummer.
There's ne'er a band in old Scotland
Could play such a tune as this.

Oh, it's old King Twine and he called for his wine,
And he called for his barbers three,
And if ever a barber could shave well,
For a very fine razor had he.
   "Oh, hold up your snoot," said the barber . . .

Oh, it's old King Twine and he called for his wine,
And he called for his farmers three,
And if ever a farmer could farm well,
For a very fine farm had he.
   "Oh, whoa, Buck, you devil," said the farmer . . .

Oh, it's old King Twine and he called for his wine,
And he called for his preachers three,
And if ever a preacher could preach well,
For a very fine sermon had he.
   "Oh, God bless us all," said the preacher . . .

Oh, it's old King Twine and he called for his wine,
And he called for his women three,
And if ever a woman could scold well,
For the devil of a tongue had she.
   "Oh, Yang! Yang! Yang!" said the woman,
   "God bless us all," said the preacher,
   "Whoa, Buck, you devil," said the farmer,

"Hold up your snoot," said the barber,
"Toodle-doodle-oo," said the fifer,
"Yank-yanky-doodle," said the fiddler,
"Rub-a-dub-a-dum," said the drummer,
There's ne'er a band in old Scotland
Could play such a tune as this.

# Charms and Omens

## Weather

**116.**

A ring around the moon,
Rain is coming soon.

**117.**

A sunshiny shower
Won't last half an hour.

**118.**

A mackerel sky,
Tomorrow's dry.

**119.**

When it rains before seven,
Shine before eleven.

**120.**

Rain, rain, go to Spain!
Never show your face again!

**121.**

Rain, rain, go away!
Come again another day.
Dot and Helen want to play.

**122.**

March winds and April showers
Bring forth May flowers.

**123.**

Red sky at night, sailors' delight,
Red sky at morning, sailors take warning.

**124.**

Rainbow at night, sailors' delight.
Rainbow in the morning, sailors take warning.

**125.**

Evening red and morning grey
Will set the traveller on his way,
But evening grey and morning red
Will pour down rain upon his head.

**126.**

The wind from the east
Is good for neither man nor beast.

**127.**

When the wind is in the north,
Then the wise fisherman goes not forth.

When the wind is in the south,
It blows the bait in the fish's mouth.

When the wind is in the east,
Then the fishing is the least.

When the wind is in the west,
Then the fishing is the best.

**128.**

As the days lengthen
So the cold strengthens.

## Wishes and Warnings

**129.**

Star white, star bright,
First star I've seen tonight,
I wish I may, I wish I might
Have the wish I wish tonight.

**130.**

See a pin and pick it up
And all that day you'll have good luck.
See a pin and let it lie
And all that day you'll have to cry.

**131.**

One crow, sorrow,
Two crows, joy,
Three crows, a wedding,
Four crows, a boy.

**132.**

Step on a crack,
Break your mother's back.

Step on a line,
Have to pay a fine.

**133.**

Wear at the toe, spend as you go.
Wear at the heel, spend a great deal.
Wear on the ball, spend it all.
Wear at the side, a gentleman's bride.

**134.**

Lucky lucky white horse,
Lucky lucky lee,
Lucky lucky white horse,
Bring my wish to me.

**135.**

One I love, two I love,
Three I love, I say.
Four I love with all my heart,
Five I cast away.
Six she loves, seven he loves,
Eight they both love.
Nine she comes, ten he tarries,
Eleven he woos, twelve, he marries.
Thirteen for riches, fourteen for stitches,
Fifteen, he tears a hole in his britches.

**136.**

Sneeze on Monday, sneeze for news,
Sneeze on Tuesday, sneeze for shoes.
Sneeze on Wednesday, sneeze for a letter,
Sneeze on Thursday, for something better.
Sneeze on Friday, sneeze for sorrow,
Sneeze on Saturday, see your true love tomorrow.
Sneeze on Sunday, your safety seek
Or the devil will have you the rest of the week.

**137.**

Friday's dream on Saturday told
Is sure to come true be it ever so old.

**138.**

Stub your toe, see your beau.
Kiss your thumb, he's sure to come.

**139.**

If you wish to live and thrive
Let a spider run alive.

**140.**

A whistling girl and a crowing hen
Always come to some bad end.

**141.**

A swarm of bees in May
Is worth a load of hay.
A swarm of bees in June
Is worth a silver spoon.
A swarm of bees in July
Is not worth a fly.

**142.**

Monday's child is fair of face,
Tuesday's child is full of grace.
Wednesday's child is full of woe,
Thursday's child has far to go.
Friday's child is loving and giving,
Saturday's child works hard for a living.
The child that is born on the Sabbath day
Is fair and wise and good and gay.

**143.**

Sing out of season,
Cry without reason.

**Weddings**

**144.**

Change the name and not the letter,
You change for worse and not for better.

**145.**

Monday for health, Tuesday for wealth,
Wednesday the best day of all.
Thursday for crosses, Friday for losses,
Saturday no day at all.

**146.**

Something old, something new,
Something borrowed, something blue,
And a new penny in your shoe.

**147.**

Married in red, you'll wish yourself dead.
Married in blue, he will always prove true.
Married in white, you've chosen all right.
Married in green, not fit to be seen.
Married in brown, you'll live out of town.
Married in black, you'll wish yourself back.
Married in grey, you'll live far away.
Married in pink, your spirits will sink.

# Curious Characters

### 148. *There Was a Crooked Man*

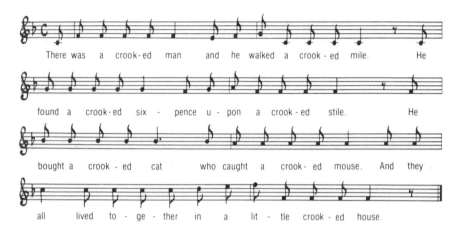

There was a crooked man and he walked a crooked mile.
He found a crooked sixpence upon a crooked stile.
He bought a crooked cat who caught a crooked mouse,
And they all lived together in a little crooked house.

### 149. *Bessy Bell and Mary Grey*

Bessy Bell and Mary Grey,
They were two bonny lassies.
They built their house upon a lea
And covered it with rushes.

## 150.  *Tommy and the Apples*

As Tom-my was walk-ing one fine sum-mer's day   Some

ro-sy cheeked ap-ples he saw on his way.   Saw on his way,

saw on his way,   Some ro-sy cheeked ap-ples he saw on his way.

As Tommy was walking one fine summer's day
Some rosy-cheeked apples he saw on his way,
Saw on his way, saw on his way,
Some rosy-cheeked apples he saw on his way.

Those apples were ripe and so pleasant to see,
They seemed to say, "Tommy, come climb up the tree,
Climb up the tree, climb up the tree."
They seemed to say, "Tommy, come climb up the tree."

So Tommy climbed up: from the bough he did fall,
And down came poor Tommy, the apples and all,
Apples and all, apples and all,
And down came poor Tommy, the apples and all.

His face was all scratched and he felt very sore.
He promised he'd never steal apples no more,
Apples no more, apples no more,
He promised he'd never steal apples no more.

## 151. *Patsy on the Railroad*

In eigh - teen hun - dred and nine - ty one I found my life had
just be - gun. I found my life had just be - gun, Work - ing on the
rail - road. Pat - sy - at - sy - o - ry ay, Pat - sy at - sy
o - ry-ay, Pat - sy at - sy o - ry-ay, Work - ing on the rail - road.!

In eighteen hundred and ninety-one
I found my life had just begun.
I found my life had just begun,
Working on the railroad.

REFRAIN:

Patsy-atsy ory-ay,
Patsy-atsy ory-ay,
Patsy-atsy ory-ay,
Working on the railroad!

In eighteen hundred and ninety-two
I found myself with nothing to do.
I found myself with nothing to do,
Working on the railroad.

In eighteen hundred and ninety-three
The American railroad hired me ...

In eighteen hundred and ninety-four
Fell on my back, was getting sore ...

In eighteen hundred and ninety-five
Found myself more dead than alive ...

In eighteen hundred and ninety-six
Sat on a keg of dynamite sticks ...

In eighteen hundred and ninety-seven
Found myself on the way to heaven ...

In eighteen hundred and ninety-eight
Found myself at the pearly gate ...

In eighteen hundred and ninety-nine
St. Peter said, "Go down the line." ...

## 152. *The Old Soldier*

Now there was an old soldier and he had a wooden leg.
He had no tobacco, no tobacco could he beg.
There was an old sailor as cunning as a fox,
And he always had tobacco in his old tobacco box.

Says the soldier to the sailor, "Give me a chew."
Says the sailor to the soldier, "I'll be hanged if I do.
Save up your old quids and dry them on the rocks,
And you'll always have tobacco in your old tobacco box."

## 153. Old Seth Coon

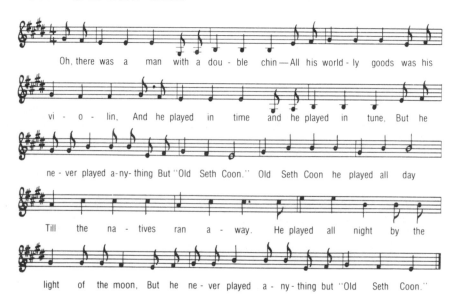

Oh, there was a man with a double chin–
All his worldly goods was his violin,
And he played in time and he played in. tune,
But he never played anything but "Old Seth Coon."

REFRAIN:

Old Seth Coon he played all day
Till the natives ran away.
He played all night by the light of the moon,
But he never played anything but "Old Seth Coon."

So they took that man with the double chin,
All his worldly goods and his violin,
And they packed him off to a foreign shore
Where the natives never heard the tune before.

Old Seth Coon he played all night
Till the natives took to flight.
He played the tune and it had no end,
And it isn't any wonder that he had no friends.

## 154. *Little Brown Jug*

Me and my wife we lived alone
In a little log hut we called our own.
She loved whisky, I liked rum,
Tell you what, we'd lots of fun.

REFRAIN:

Ha ha ha, you and me,
Little brown jug, don't I love thee!
Ha ha ha, you and me,
Little brown jug, don't I love thee!

93

When I go strolling round my farm
Take little brown jug under my arm.
Place her under a shady tree,
No one there but her and me.

Aunt Maria had a horse,
She kept it in the barn of course.
She fed it on both oats and hay,
And rode it round the farm all day.

Uncle Abner had a still,
He kept it high upon a hill.
The heavens howled and the thunder roared,
And Uncle Abner yelled for more.

### 155.  *Johnny Went Down in the Bucket*

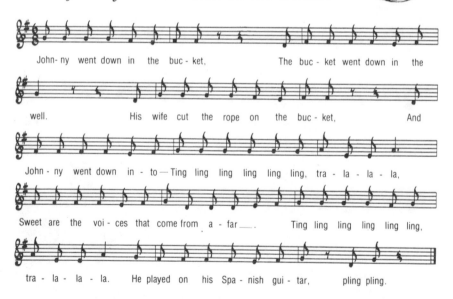

John-ny went down in the buc-ket, The buc-ket went down in the well. His wife cut the rope on the buc-ket, And John-ny went down in-to—Ting ling ling ling ling ling, tra-la-la-la, Sweet are the voi-ces that come from a-far___. Ting ling ling ling ling ling, tra-la-la-la. He played on his Spa-nish gui-tar, pling pling.

Johnny went down in the bucket,
The bucket went down in the well.

His wife cut the rope on the bucket,
And Johnny went down into–
    Ting ling ling ling, tra la la,
    Sweet are the voices that come from afar.
    Ting ling ling ling, tra la la,
    He played on his Spanish guitar, pling pling.

Johnny went down into Hades.
He hit with a terrible wham
Right on a red-hot shovel
And started to curse with a–
    Ting ling ling ling, tra la la,
    Sweet are the voices that come from afar.
    Ting ling ling ling, tra la la,
    He played on his Spanish guitar, pling pling.

The Devil he heard him a-cussing
And slapped him right into a cell.
Said he, "I'm a jolly good fellow,
But I won't have no cussing in–
    Ting ling ling ling, tra la la,
    Sweet are the voices that come from afar.
    Ting ling ling ling, tra la la,
    He played on his Spanish guitar, pling pling.


## 156. *Three Wise Old Women*

Three wise old women were they, were they,
Who went to hunt on a winter's day.
One carried a ladder to climb for plums;
One carried a basket to hold some gums;
The third – and she was the silliest one–
She carried a fan to keep off the sun.

"Dear, dear," said one, "A bear I see.
I think we'd better all climb a tree."
But there were no trees for miles around
So far too frightened to stay on the ground,
They climbed their ladder right up to the top,
And sat there screaming, "We'll drop! We'll drop."

The wind was high as the wind could be
And carried their ladder right out to sea,
And soon the old women were all afloat
In a leaky old ladder instead of a boat,
And every time that the waves rolled in
Of course the poor things they were wet to the skin.

They took their basket and tried to bail,
They put their fan up to make a sail,
But whether they ever got home or no,
Or whether they saw any bears, oh ho,
Why you must ask them – for I don't know.

### 157.  *There Once Was a Maiden*

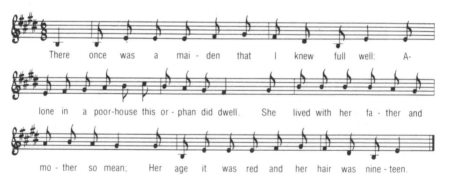

There once was a maiden that I knew full well:
Alone in a poorhouse this orphan did dwell.
She lived with her father and mother so mean;
Her age it was red and her hair was nineteen.

Now she had a lover who close by did dwell:
He was cross-eyed in both feet and humpbacked as well,
Saying, "Come fly with me by the light of yon star
For the eye of my apple you are."

"Oh, no," said the maiden, "Now gently be wise.
My father would scratch out your nails with his eyes,
And if you love me don't bring me disgrace,"
Cried the maid as she buried her hands in her face.

Now as soon as he heard this he knocked down this maid
And quickly he opened the knife of his blade.
Then he cut the throat of this damsel so fair,
And he dragged her around by the head of her hair.

Unseen at this moment her father appears
And gazed on his daughter with eyes in his tears.
Then he grabbed this base villain by the hands with
    his throat,
An he shot him with a horse pistol raised from a colt.

## 158. *Maverick the Two-Gun Cowboy*

TUNE: RUDOLPH THE RED-NOSED REINDEER

Maverick the Two-Gun Cowboy had a very shiny gun,
And if you ever saw it, it would even make you run.
All of the other cowboys used to laugh and call him names.
They would never let poor Maverick join in any poker games.
Then one foggy Christmas Eve the sheriff came to say:
"Maverick with your gun so bright
Won't you shoot my wife tonight?"
Then how all the cowboys loved him, and they shouted out
    with glee:
"Maverick the Two-Gun Cowboy, you'll go down in
    history!"

## 159. *A Gallant Ship*

About the year of one, two, three
A gallant ship went out to sea
To catch a whale by the end of its tail,
Put salt on the end of its tail.
And when about a mile from shore
The ship began to dance,
And every son of a sailorman
Put on his working pants,
His pants, his pants, his working trousers.

And down into the hole they went
And to the pump their backs they bent.
It was so wet they couldn't sit down,
So wet they couldn't sit down.
Then up spoke Michael Flaherty:
"A Jonah's on the boat," said he,
So they downed the pumps and away they ran
To find the Jonah man.

And way up in the middle of the deck
The smiling Jonah sat,
Smoking a paper cigarette
In the crown of his derby hat,
His hat, his hat, get on to that.
So they gave a heave and they gave a yell
And overboard poor Jonah fell,
And they sent him along and they wished him well,
And there's nothing more to tell.

### 160.  *A Leg of Mutton Went Over to France*

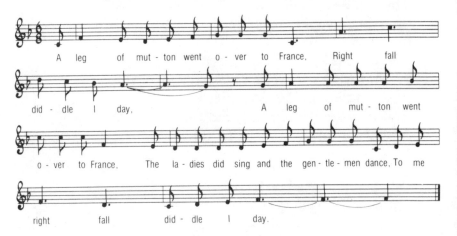

A leg of mutton went over to France,
    Right fall diddle I day,
A leg of mutton went over to France,
The ladies did sing and the gentlemen dance,
    To me right fall diddle I day.

There was a man and he was dead,
    Right fall diddle I day,
There was a man and he was dead,
They sent for a doctor to look in his head,
    To me right fall diddle I day.

And in his head there was a spring ...
Where thirty-nine salmon were learning to sing ...

And near the spring there was a pool ...
Where all the young salmon they went to school ...

Oh, one of them was as big as I ...
Perhaps you might think I am singing a lie ...

Oh, one of them was small as an elf ...
If you want any more you can sing it yourself ...

## 161.  *The Rich Man and the Poor Man*

There was a rich man and he lived in Jerusalem,
    Glory hallelujah, hi-ro-jerum.
He wore a silk hat and his coat was very sprucium,
    Glory hallelujah, hi-ro-jerum.

REFRAIN:

Hi-ro-jerum, hi-ro-jerum,
Skinna ma linka too-li-um,
Skinna ma linka too-li-um,
Glory hallelujah, hi-ro-jerum.

One day to his door there came a human wreckium,
    Glory hallelujah, hi-ro-jerum.

He wore a bowler hat and the brim was round his neckium,
  Glory hallelujah, hi-ro-jerum.

The poor man begged for a piece of bread and cheesium ...
The rich man said he'd call for a policium ...

The poor man died and his soul went to heavium ...
He danced with the angels till a quarter past elevium ...

The rich man died but he didn't fare so wellium ...
He couldn't get to heaven so he had to go to hellium ...

The moral of this story is riches are no jokium ...
We'll all go to heaven 'cause we're all stony brokium ...

## 162. Old Adam

I'm so sor - ry for old A - dam. Just as sor - ry as can be. 'Cause he ne - ver had a mam - my For to rock him on her knee.

I'm so sorry for old Adam,
Just as sorry as can be,
'Cause he never had a mammy
For to rock him on her knee,

And he never had a daddy
For to tell him all he knowed,
And he never had nobody
To point out the narrow road,

And he never had no childhood
Playing round the cabin door,

And he never had a mammy
For to snatch him off the floor,

And he never had a feeling
When he laid him down to rest
Of the 'possum and the taties
Tucked beneath his little vest,

And I've always had a feeling
He'd have let that apple be
If he'd only had a mammy
For to rock him on her knee.

### 163. *I Was Born About Four Thousand Years Ago*

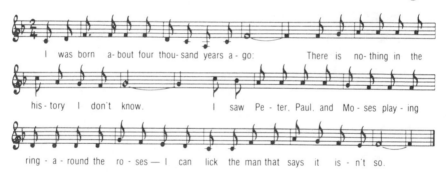

I was born about four thousand years ago:
There is nothing in the history I don't know.
I saw Peter, Paul, and Moses playing ring-around-the-roses–
I can lick the man that says it isn't so.

I saw Eve and Adam driven from the door;
It was I who picked the fig leaves that they wore.
When the apple they were eating I was round the corner
      peeking,
And I'll swear that I'm the guy that ate the core.

I saw Caesar when he crossed the Rubicon;
It was I who built the raft he crossed it on.
I saw Jonah swallow the whale, and I pulled the lion's tail,
And when I looked for Daniel, he was gone.

I saw Absalom a-hanging by the hair.
When they built the wall in China I was there.
Once I saved King Solomon's life and he offered me a wife;
I said, "Now you're talking business; take a chair."

Oh, the Queen of Sheba fell in love with me;
We were married in Milwaukee secretly,
But in Washington I shook 'er just to join with
    General Hooker,
Chasing skeeters out of lazy Tennessee.

I'm the guy that owned the mare Godiva rode;
It's a lie that just her hair was all that showed.
When she mounted for the ride I was standing by her side,
And I could see her legs were badly bowed.

I saw Samson when he laid the village cold.
I can prove that good Queen Bess was very bold.
I helped build the tower of Babel up as high as they were able,
And there's lots of other things I haven't told.

# Dopey Ditties

**164.**

Goodnight, sleep tight.
Don't let the bedbugs bite.
If they do, get your shoe
And hit them till they're black and blue.

**165.**

A peanut sat on a railway track–
Its heart was all a-flutter.
Around the bend came a railroad train–
"Toot! Toot!" – Peanut butter.

**166.**

One fine night in the middle of May
A curious stranger lost his way.
He saw a sign – it was dark and faint–
He climbed to the top, and it said "Wet paint."

**167.**

One bright morning in the middle of the night
Two dead boys got up to fight.
Back to back they faced each other,
Drew their swords and shot each other.
A deaf policeman heard the noise,
Came and shot those two dead boys.
If you don't believe my lies are true,
Ask the blind man, he saw it too.

**168.**

I have a little brown cow,
It gives me milk and cheese.

Here I sit in my bedroom
With hoof and mouth disease.

**169.**

TUNE: THERE IS A HAPPY LAND

There is a boarding school
Far, far away
Where they get onion soup
Three times a day.
Oh, how the boarders yell
When they hear the dinner bell!
Oh, how those onions smell
Three times a day!

**170.**

O hell, O hell, O Helen, do be mine!
Your feet, your feet, your features are divine.
I swear, I swear, I swear that I'll be true.
O damn, O damn, O damsel, I love you.

**171.**

You've got bats in your belfry that flut.
Your comprenez-vous cord is cut.
There's nobody home in the top of your dome—
Your head's not a head, it's a nut.

**172.**

If-icky I-icky
Had-icky my-icky
Gun-icky I-icky
Would-icky shoot-icky

Yon-icky swan-icky
In-icky yon-icky
Mill-icky dam-icky.

**173.**

TUNE: ALOUETTE

Suffocation! This is suffocation!
Suffocation! Easy game to play.
First you get a plastic bag,
Then you put it on your head,
Go to bed, wake up dead,
Weee – eee – eee.

**174.**

TUNE: THE WEE LAMBIE (NO. 69)

An awful black eye has my Uncle Jim.
Somebody threw a tomato at him.
"Tomatoes can't hurt you," I said with a grin.
Oh, yes, they can, when they're still in the tin.

## 175. *The Hearse Song*

Did you ever think when you see a hearse
That some day you'll be as bad or worse?
They'll take you away in a big black hack;
They'll take you away, but they won't bring you back.
    A-woo--oo! A-woo-oo!

They'll take you out and they'll lower you down;
They'll shovel you into that cold, cold ground.
They'll throw in dirt, and they'll throw in rocks,
And they won't give a damn if they break the box ...

The worms crawl out and the worms crawl in;
They crawl all over your mouth and chin.
Your eyes drop out and your teeth fall in,
And your limbs drop off of you, limb by limb ...

The worms crawl in and the worms crawl out;
They crawl in thin and they crawl out stout.
They invite their friends and their friends' friends too,
And you look like hell when they're through with you ...

# Answer Back Songs

## 176. Billy Boy

"Where have you been, Billy boy, Billy boy?
Where have you been, charming Billy?"
"I've been to see my wife, she's the pride of my life,
She's a young thing; she cannot leave her mother."

"Did she bid you to come in, Billy boy, Billy boy?
Did she bid you to come in, charming Billy?"
"Yes, she bid me to come in, with a dimple in her chin.
She's a young thing; she cannot leave her mother."

"Did she give to you a chair, Billy boy, Billy boy?
Did she give to you a chair, charming Billy?"
"Yes, she gave to me a chair, combing down her yellow hair.
She's a young thing; she cannot leave her mother."

"Can she bake a cherry pie, Billy boy, Billy boy?
Can she bake a cherry pie, charming Billy?"
"She can bake a cherry pie quick as a cat can wink its eye.
She's a young thing; she cannot leave her mother."

"Can she make a feather bed, Billy boy, Billy boy?
Can she make a feather bed, charming Billy?"
"She can make a feather bed, put the pillows at its head.
She's a young thing; she cannot leave her mother."

"How old is she, Billy boy, Billy boy?
How old is she, charming Billy?"
"Three times six, four times seven, twice twenty and eleven.
She's a young thing; she cannot leave her mother."

## 177. *My Boy Willie*

"Where have you been all the day, my boy Willie?
Where have you been all the day, Willie, won't you tell me
    now?"
"I've been all the day courting of my lady gay,
But she is too young to be taken from her Nanny."

"Can she pick and can she spin, my boy Willie?
Can she pick and can she spin, Willie, won't you tell me now?"
"She can pick and she can spin and she can do most anything,
But she is too young to be taken from her Nanny."

"Can she brew and can she bake, my boy Willie?
Can she brew and can she bake, Willie, won't you tell me
 now?"
"She can brew and she can bake and she can make a wedding
 cake,
But she is too young to be taken from her Nanny."

"How old is she now, my boy Willie?
How old is she now, Willie, won't you tell me now?"
"Twice six, twice seven, twice twenty and eleven,
But she is too young to be taken from her Nanny."

### 178. *Henery, My Boy*

"Where have you been all day, He-ne-ry, He-ne-ry, my boy, He-ne-ry, my boy, He-ne-ry my boy?" "Down to sis-ter's, down to sis-ter's. Make my bed, Maw, for I want to lay down."

"Where have you been all day, Henery, Henery, my boy,
Henery, my boy, Henery, my boy?"
"Down to sister's, down to sister's.
Make my bed, Maw, for I want to lay down."

"What did you have, down to sister's, Henery,
 Henery, my boy,
Henery, my boy, Henery, my boy?"
"Tea with p'ison, tea with p'ison.
Make my bed, Maw, for I want to lay down."

113

### 179. A Paper of Pins

"I'll give to you a pa-per of pins, For that's the way my love be-gins, If you will mar-ry me, miss, If you will mar-ry me."

"I'll give to you a paper of pins,
  For that's the way my love begins,
  If you will marry me, miss,
  If you will marry me."

"I'll not accept the paper of pins
  If that's the way your love begins,
  For I'll not marry you, sir,
  I'll not marry you."

"I'll give to you a dress of red
  All bound around with golden thread,
  If you will marry me, miss,
  If you will marry me."

"I'll not accept the dress of red
  All bound around with golden thread,
  For I'll not marry you, sir,
  I'll not marry you."

"I'll give to you the key of my heart
  That you and I may never part,
  If you will marry me, miss,
  If you will marry me."

"I'll not accept the key of your heart
  That you and I may never part,
  For I'll not marry you, sir,
  I'll not marry you."

"I'll give to you the key of my chest
  That you may have money at your request,
  If you will marry me, miss,
  If you will marry me."

"I will accept the key of your chest
  That I may have money at my request,
  For I will marry you, sir,
  I will marry you."

"You'll not accept the key of my chest
  That you may have money at your request,
  For I'll not have you now, miss,
  I'll not have you now."

## 180.   *Where Are You Going, My Pretty Maid?*

Where are you going, my pretty maid, my pretty maid?
Where are you going, my pretty maid?
"I'm going a-milking, sir," she said, "sir," she said.
"I'm going a-milking, sir," she said.

May I go with you, my pretty maid, my pretty maid?
May I go with you, my pretty maid?
"If you are kind, sir," she said, "sir," she said.
"If you are kind, sir," she said.

What is your father, my pretty maid, my pretty maid?
What is your father, my pretty maid?
"My father's a farmer, sir," she said, "sir," she said.
"My father's a farmer, sir," she said.

What is your fortune, my pretty maid, my pretty maid?
What is your fortune, my pretty maid?
"My face is my fortune, sir," she said, "sir," she said.
"My face is my fortune, sir," she said.

Then I'll not have you, my pretty maid, my pretty maid.
Then I'll not have you, my pretty maid.
"Nobody asked you, sir," she said, "sir," she said.
"Nobody asked you, sir," she said.

## 181. *No, Sir*

"Tell me one thing, tell me tru-ly, Tell me why you scorn me so.

Tell me why, when asked a ques-tion, You will al-ways an-swer no."

"No, sir, no, sir, no sir, no!" ("My . . .)

"Tell me one thing, tell me truly,
Tell me why you scorn me so.
Tell me why, when asked a question,
You will always answer no."
    "No, sir, no, sir, no, sir, no!

"My father was a Spanish merchant
And before he sailed away
He told me to be sure and answer
No to all you'd do and say.
    No, sir, no, sir, no, sir, no!"

"If while walking in a garden
Plucking flowers all wet with dew,
Tell me, would you be offended
If I walked and talked with you?"
    "No, sir, no, sir, no, sir, no!"

"If while walking in the garden
I should ask you to be mine,
And should tell you that I love you,
Would you then my heart decline?"
    "No, sir, no, sir, no, sir, no!"

## 182.  *Soldier, Soldier, Will You Marry Me?*

O sol - dier, sol - dier will you mar-ry me, With your mus-ket, fife and
drum?" "O no, sweet maid, I can- not mar- ry thee For I have no coat to put
on." So up she climbed to her grand - fa - ther's chest And she
brought him a coat of the ve - ry ve - ry best. And the sol - dier put it on.

"O soldier, soldier, will you marry me,
With your musket, fife, and drum?"
"O no, sweet maid, I cannot marry thee
For I have no coat to put on."
   So up she climbed to her grandfather's chest
   And she brought him a coat of the very very best,
   And the soldier put it on.

"O soldier, soldier, will you marry me,
With your musket, fife, and drum?"
"O no, sweet maid, I cannot marry thee
For I have no shoes to put on."
   So up she climbed to her grandfather's chest
   And she brought him some shoes of the very very best,
   And the soldier put them on.

"O soldier, soldier, will you marry me,
With your musket, fife, and drum?"
"O no, sweet maid, I cannot marry thee
For I have no hat to put on."

So up she climbed to her grandfather's chest
And she brought him a hat of the very very best,
And the soldier put it on.

"O soldier, soldier, will you marry me,
With your musket, fife, and drum?"
"O no, sweet maid, I cannot marry thee
For I have no pants to put on."
So up she climbed to her grandfather's chest
And she brought him some pants of the very very best,
And the soldier put them on.

"O soldier, soldier, will you marry me,
With your musket, fife, and drum?"
"O no, sweet maid, I cannot marry thee
For I have a wife of my own."

## 183. *Madam, I Have Come to Court*

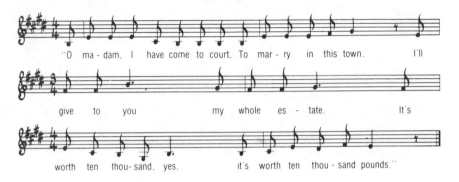

"O ma-dam, I have come to court. To mar-ry in this town. I'll give to you my whole es-tate. It's worth ten thou-sand. yes. it's worth ten thou-sand pounds."

"O madam, I have come to court,
 To marry in this town.
 I'll give to you my whole estate,
 It's worth ten thousand, yes, it's worth ten thousand
  pounds."

"O kind sir, you have come to court,
 To marry in this town,
 And I don't want your whole estate,
 It's worth ten thousand, yes, it's worth ten thousand
  pounds."

"O madam, I have a very fine house,
 It's newly erectified,
 And you may have it for yourself
 If you will be my bride, yes, if you will be my bride."

"O kind sir, you have a very fine house
 That's newly erectified,
 But you may have it for yourself
 For I will not be your bride, no, I will not be your bride."

"O madam, I have a very fine horse
 And his face is like the vine,

And you may have him for yourself
If you will be but mine, yes, if you will be but mine."

"O kind sir, you have a very fine horse
And his face is like the vine.
His master likes a glass of wine
And I'm afraid his horse might learn, yes, I'm afraid
    his horse might learn."

"O madam, I have a lot of land,
It's four score acres wide,
And you may have it for yourself
If you will be my bride, yes, if you will be my bride."

"O kind sir, you have a lot of land
With pastures at the foot,
And if you were in I'd turn you out
For I know a hog would root, yes, I know a hog would root."

"O madam, you're a scornful dame
And a very hard one to please.
When you grow old and chilled with the cold,
I hope I see you freeze, yes, I hope I see you freeze."

"When I grow old and chilled with the cold
'Twon't be you that will keep me warm,
So when I'm free please let me be
And I'll keep myself from harm, yes, I'll keep myself
    from harm."

## 184. *Madam, I Have Come A-courting*

"Madam, I have come a-court-ing If your fa-vour
I might gain. If you'll free-ly en-ter-tain me. Oh, per-haps I'll call a-gain."
Da-di-um, a-der - ry, a-der-ry, a-der-ry. Da-di-um, a-der - ry, a-der-ry, a-day.

"Madam, I have come a-courting
If your favour I might gain.
If you'll freely entertain me,
Oh, perhaps I'll call again."

REFRAIN:

Da-di-um, a-derry, a-derry, a-derry,
Da-di-um, a-derry, a-derry a-day.

"Blue it is a handsome colour
Till it gets a second dip,
Like young men when they go a-courting
Very often make a slip."

"Madam, I have gold and silver,
Madam, I have houses and land.
Madam, I have worldly treasure–
All will be at your command."

"What care I for your gold or silver?
What care I for your houses or land?
What care I for worldly treasure?
All I want is a handsome young man."

"The biggest apple soon grows rotten,
  The hottest love soon grows cold.
  Young men's words are soon forgotten.
  Pretty fair maid, don't speak so bold."

"A handsome man I do admire,
  A handsome man I do adore.
  A handsome man I mean to marry,
  Be him rich or be him poor."

"Madam, you are very saucy,
  Madam, you are hard to please.
  Madam, you are very saucy–
  I hope to the Lord that you will freeze."

# Love . . . and Marriage

## 185. *Lavender's Blue*

La - ven - der's blue, dil - ly - dil - ly, la - ven - der's green, If I were
king, dil - ly - dil - ly, I'd need a queen. Who told me so, dil - ly - dil - ly,
who told me so? 'Twas my own heart, dil - ly - dil - ly, that told me so.

Lavender's blue, dilly-dilly, lavender's green,
If I were king, dilly-dilly, I'd need a queen.
Who told me so, dilly-dilly, who told me so?
'Twas my own heart, dilly-dilly, that told me so.

Call out your men, dilly-dilly, put them to work,
Some with a rake, dilly-dilly, some with a fork,
Some to make hay, dilly-dilly, some to plant corn,
While you and I, dilly-dilly, keep ourselves warm.

If it should hap, dilly-dilly, if it should chance,
Then we'd be gay, dilly-dilly, and we'd all dance.
Lavender's blue, dilly-dilly, lavender's green,
When I am king, dilly-dilly, you'll be my queen.

## 186. Johnny's So Long at the Fair

O dear, what can the mat-ter be? Dear, dear, what can the mat-ter be?

O dear, what can the mat-ter be? John-ny's so long at the fair.

REFRAIN:

O dear, what can the matter be?
Dear, dear, what can the matter be?
O dear, what can the matter be?
Johnny's so long at the fair.

He promised to buy me a fairing to please me,
And then for a kiss, oh, he promised to tease me.
He promised to buy me a bunch of blue ribbons
To tie up my bonny brown hair.

He promised to buy me a basket of posies,
A garland of lilies, a garland of roses,
A little straw hat to set off the blue ribbons
That tie up my bonny brown hair.

## 187. New River Train

Leav-ing on that New Ri-ver Train, Leav-ing on that New Ri-ver Train,

Same old train that brought me here Gon-na car-ry me back a - gain.

Dar - ling, you can't love but one. Dar - ling, you can't love but one.

Can't love but one and have a - ny fun. No, my dar- ling, you can't love but one.

Leaving on that New River Train,
Leaving on that New River Train,
Same old train that brought me here
Going to carry me back again.

Darling, you can't love but one.
Darling, you can't love but one.
Can't love but one and have any fun.
No, my darling, you can't love but one.

Darling, you can't love two.
Darling, you can't love two.
You can't love two and your little heart be true.
No, my darling, you can't love two.

Darling, you can't love three.
Darling, you can't love three.
You can't love three and keep your love of me.
No, my darling, you can't love three.

Darling, you can't love four.
Darling, you can't love four.
You can't love four and love me any more.
No, my darling, you can't love four.

Darling, you can't love five.
Darling, you can't love five.
You can't love five and keep our love alive.
No, my darling, you can't love five.

Now darling, remember what you said.
Darling, remember what you said.
Remember that you said you would rather see me dead
Than leaving on that New River Train.

But I'm leaving on that New River Train,
Leaving on that New River Train.
Same old train that brought me here
Going to carry me back again.

## 188. *Rattle on the Stovepipe*

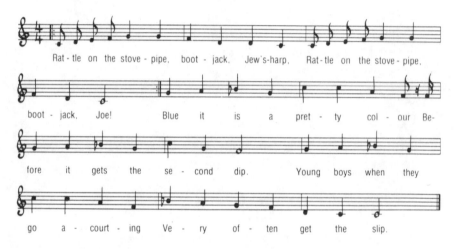

Rat-tle on the stove-pipe, boot-jack, Jew's-harp. Rat-tle on the stove-pipe, boot-jack, Joe! Blue it is a pret-ty col-our Be-fore it gets the se-cond dip. Young boys when they go a-court-ing Ve-ry of-ten get the slip.

REFRAIN:

Rattle on the stovepipe, bootjack, Jew's-harp,
Rattle on the stovepipe, bootjack, Joe!
Rattle on the stovepipe, bootjack, Jew's-harp,
Rattle on the stovepipe, bootjack, Joe!

Blue it is a pretty colour
Before it gets the second dip.
Young boys when they go a-courting
Very often get the slip.

Ripest apples soon grow rotten,
Hottest love will soon grow cold.
Pretty fair maids are soon forgotten,
I pray young man, don't be so bold.

She was kissing, I was wishing,
Didn't know what she was about.
Robbed me of my gold and silver,
Then she kicked me, threw me out.

Deepest water running swiftly,
Birds a-flying through the air,
Kiss the young men, go a-courting,
Kind sir, I don't have a care.

### 189. *I Took a Notion Now*

Early one morning, the weather being fair,
The father and the son walked out to take the air,
And as they were a-walking the son began to vow:
"I must and will get married for I took a notion now."

"O son, dear son, just hold your idle tongue,
For you to talk of marriage, I fear you're far too young."

"My age is sixteen and that you must allow.
I must and will get married for I took a notion now."

"Oh, what if you should try and couldn't get a wife?"
"O father, there's no danger, for there is Liza Fife.
Her age is sixteen and that you must allow.
I must and will get married for I took a notion now."

"Oh, what if she did slight you as you did her before?"
"O father, there's no danger for there are plenty more.
There's Margaret and there's Jane and the girl that tends the
    cow.
I must and will get married for I took a notion now."

## 190. Common Bill

I'll tell you of a fellow, of a fellow I have seen: He's
neither white nor yellow, nor yet so very green. His
name it isn't charming for it's only common Bill. He
wishes me to wed him, but I hardly think I will. He
wishes me to wed him, but I hardly think I will.

I'll tell you of a fellow, of a fellow I have seen:
He's neither white nor yellow, nor yet so very green.

His name it isn't charming for it's only common Bill.
He wishes me to wed him, but I hardly think I will.
He wishes me to wed him, but I hardly think I will.

Last night he came to see me, but he made so long a stay ·
I began to think the fellow never meant to go away.
He said, "Wouldn't it be pleasant as we journey up the hill
To go hand in hand together?" But I hardly think I will.
"To go hand in hand together?" But I hardly think I will.

He tells me of devotion, of devotion true and deep.
It sounds so very silly that I almost go to sleep.
He says through storm and sunshine he will truly love
    me still.
He wishes me to wed him, but I hardly think I will.
He wishes me to wed him, but I hardly think I will.

I'm sure I would not choose him, but the very deuce is in it.
He says if I refuse him he cannot live a minute,
And you know the blessed Bible says it's very wrong to kill,
So I've thought the matter over, and I guess I'll marry Bill.
So I've thought the matter over, and I guess I'll marry Bill.

### 191. My Grandma

Oh, my Grand - ma lived on yon - der vil - lage green, As
fine an old la - dy as e - ver was seen. But she
of - ten cau - tioned me with care Of all false young men —

Oh, my Grandma lived on yonder village green,
As fine an old lady as ever was seen,
But she often cautioned me with care
Of all false young men to beware.
    Ti-me-I ti-me-um-tum, ti-me-um-ta-ta,
    Of all false young men to beware.
    Ti-me-I ti-me-um-tum, ti-me-um-ta-ta,
    Of all false young men to beware.

Now the first to come a-courting was little Johnny Green,
As fine a young fellow as ever was seen,
But the words of my Grandma echoed in my head,
I couldn't hear one word he said.
    Ti-me-I ti-me-um-tum, ti-me-um-ta-ta,
    I couldn't hear one word he said.
    Ti-me-I ti-me-um-tum, ti-me-um-ta-ta,
    I couldn't hear one word he said.

And the next to come a-courting was little Johnny Dove.
Here I met with a joyous love.
With a joyous love I needn't be afraid:
It's better to get married than to die an old maid ...

Ah, says I to myself, there's surely some mistake.
What a fuss these old folk make!
If the boys and the girls had always been afraid,
My Grandmama herself would have died an old maid ...

## 192.  *Tying Apples on a Lilac Tree*

A little boy and a little girl
In an ecstasy of bliss,
Said the little boy to the little girl,
"Pray give me just one kiss."
The girl drew back in great surprise:
"You're a stranger, sir," said she,

"But I will give you but just one kiss
When the apples grow on a lilac tree."

The boy felt very sad at heart:
She was his only one,
And the girl felt great remorse
At the terrible wrong she had done,
So bright and early on the very next morn,
He was quite surprised to see
His little sweetheart standing in the garden,
Tying apples on a lilac tree.

## 193.  *The Bonny Wee Window*

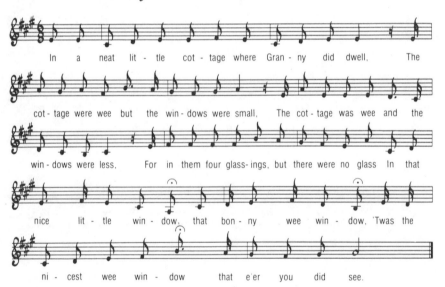

In a neat lit - tle cot - tage where Gran - ny did dwell, The
cot - tage were wee but the win - dows were small, The cot - tage was wee and the
win - dows were less, For in them four glass - ings, but there were no glass In that
nice lit - tle win - dow, that bon - ny wee win - dow, 'Twas the
ni - cest wee win - dow that e'er you did see.

In a neat little cottage where Granny did dwell,
The cottage were wee but the windows were small,
The cottage was wee and the windows were less,
For in them four glassings, but there was no glass
    In that nice little window, that bonny wee window,
    'Twas the nicest wee window that e'er you did see.

One evening when Granny had gone to her bed
And Johnny, the dearest lad young Nelly had,
Came over the hills young Nelly to woo,
Saying, "What wouldn't love make a fond lover do?"
　　With his head at the window, the bonny wee window,
　　'Twas the nicest wee window that e'er you did see.

Says Johnny to Nelly, "Don't take it amiss,
But before I go I will get a sweet kiss."
So to get that sweet kiss, sure he put his head through,
Saying, "What wouldn't love make a fond lover do?"
　　With his head in the window, the bonny wee window,
　　'Twas the nicest wee window that e'er you did see.

Oh, great was the kiss but better the smack,
But to Nelly's delight he couldn't get his head back,
So he ripped and he tore, he swore and he cursed,
While Nelly with laughing was ready to burst,
　　With John's head in the window, the bonny wee window,
　　'Twas the nicest wee window that e'er you did see.

Granny, hearing the noise, she jumped out on the floor,
And seizing the poker made haste for the door,
And on Johnny's back such blows she laid on,
Sure another like that would have broke his backbone,
　　And his head in the window, the bonny wee window,
　　'Twas the nicest wee window that e'er you did see.

As Johnny got free from the window once more,
Says, "The next time I kiss, sure I'll kiss through a door,
And the next time I visit, let it hail, snow, or rain,
I never will kiss through a window again."
　　Through a nice little window, a bonny wee window,
　　'Twas the nicest wee window that e'er you did see.

## 194. The Grey Mare

Young Roger was a butcher, came a-courting a maid, / rich merchant's daughter named beautiful Kate, / And she to her fortune had / jewels and rings. And she to her fortune had many fine things, And / she to her fortune had money and pounds, And a / rich store of treasures, A rich store of treasures, and twenty silk gowns.

Young Roger was a butcher, came a-courting a maid,
A rich merchant's daughter named beautiful Kate,
And she to her fortune had jewels and rings,
And she to her fortune had many fine things,
And she to her fortune had money and pounds,
And a rich store of treasures,
A rich store of treasures, and twenty silk gowns.

So the day was appointed and the money all there,
When up spoke this young man who's now in despair:
"I know she's your daughter, your daughter so fair,
But now I won't have her without the grey mare,
But now I won't have her,
But now I won't have her without the grey mare."

Oh, the money was then quickly put out of sight,
And likewise pretty Katy, his joy and delight,

And then this young man was conveyed to the door,
And they told him to never go there any more.
He pulled down his cap on his long wavy hair,
And he wished he had never,
No, he wished he had never spoke of the grey mare.

In three weeks after or somewhere about
He met this young damsel one day walking out.
"Oh, do you not know me, my darling?" said he.
"If I'm not mistaken, I have seen you," said she,
"Or some tall man like you with long wavy hair
Who once came a-courting,
Who once came a-courting my father's grey mare."

"Oh, no, pretty Katy, pretty Katy by name,
I once came a-courting, came a-courting the same,
But I thought your old father would have no dispute
For to give me his daughter and the grey mare to boot,
For to give me his daughter,
For to give me his daughter and the grey mare to boot."

"Now the men in this town should be drove to despair
For to marry a girl for the price of a mare,
But the price of a mare is never so great,
So fare you well, Roger, go mourning for Kate.
So fare you well, Roger,
So fare you well, Roger, go mourning for Kate."

## 195. *The Old Man in the Wood*

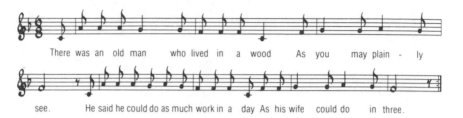

There was an old man who lived in a wood  As you may plainly see.  He said he could do as much work in a day  As his wife could do in three.

There was an old man who lived in a wood
As you may plainly see.
He said he could do as much work in a day
As his wife could do in three.

"With all my heart," the old woman said,
"If that you will allow.
Tomorrow you stay at home in my stead
And I'll go drive the plow.

"But you must mind the speckled hen
For fear she'll lay away,
And you must reel the spool of yarn
That I spun yesterday."

The old woman took the staff in her hand
And went to drive the plow.
The old man took the pail in his hand
And went to milk the cow.

But Tidy hinched and Tidy flinched
And Tidy broke his nose,
And Tidy gave him such a blow
The blood ran down to his toes.

"Hi, Tidy, hi! Hi, Tidy, ho!
Hi, Tidy, do stand still!

If ever I milk you, Tidy, again,
'Twill be sore against my will."

He went to feed the little pigs
That were within the sty.
He hit his head against the beam,
And made the blood to fly.

He went to mind the speckled hen
For fear she'd lay away,
But he forgot the spool of yarn
His wife spun yesterday.

So he cried to the sun and the moon and the stars
And the green leaves on the tree,
"If my wife doesn't do a day's work in my life
She'll never be ruled by me."

## 196. *I Wish I Was Single Again*

When I was sin-gle, O then, O then, When I was sin-gle, O then. When I was sin-gle, how the mo-ney did jin-gle, And the world went jol - ly with me then.

When I was single, O then, O then,
When I was single, O then,
When I was single, how the money did jingle,
And the world went jolly with me then.

    O the world went jolly with me then,
    O the world went jolly with me then.
    When I was single, how the money did jingle,
    And the world went jolly with me then.

I married a wife, O then, O then,
I married a wife, O then.
I married a wife, she's the plague of my life,
And I wish I was single again.

    O I wish I was single again,
    O I wish I was single again.
    I married a wife, she's the plague of my life,
    And I wish I was single again.

My wife she died, O then, O then,
My wife she died, O then.
My wife she died but I never cried,
And the world went jolly with me then.

    O the world went jolly with me then,
    O the world went jolly with me then.
    My wife she died but I never cried,
    And the world went jolly with me then.

I married another, O then, O then,
I married another, O then.
I married another, she was worse than the tother,
And I wish I was single again.

O I wish I was single again,
O I wish I was single again.
I married another, she was worse than the tother,
And I wish I was single again.

## 197. *When I Was Single*

When I was single, living at my ease,
But now I am married, a husband to please.
Four little children to maintain—
Oh, how I wish I was single again!

All those young men go flirting about the town—
You'd think they were worth a hundred thousand pound,
But search in their pockets, not a cent you will find,
So false and so fickle are those young men's minds.

But when those young men first begin to love,
It's nothing but "My honey" and "My little turtle dove,"
But when they get married, it is no such a thing—
"Get up and get the breakfast, you dirty, lazy, thing!"

## 198. Devilish Mary

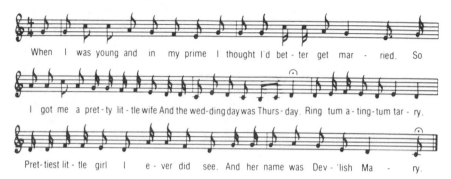

When I was young and in my prime I thought I'd bet-ter get mar - ried. So
I got me a pret-ty lit-tle wife And the wed-ding day was Thurs-day. Ring tum a-ting-tum tar - ry.
Pret-tiest lit-tle girl I e-ver did see. And her name was Dev-'lish Ma - ry.

When I was young and in my prime
I thought I'd better get married,
So I got me a pretty little wife
And the wedding day was Thursday.

REFRAIN:

Ring-tum a-ting-tum tarry,
Prettiest little girl I ever did see,
And her name was Devilish Mary.

We'd just been married about six weeks
When she got as mean as the devil,
And every time I looked cross-eyed,
She hit me on the head with a shovel.

She washed my clothes in old soapsuds,
She scratched my back with switches,
She let me know I had to mind
And she was going to wear the britches.

We'd just been married about ten weeks
When she thought we'd better be parted,
So she up with her little duds
And down the road she started.

142

## 199. Nickety Nackety

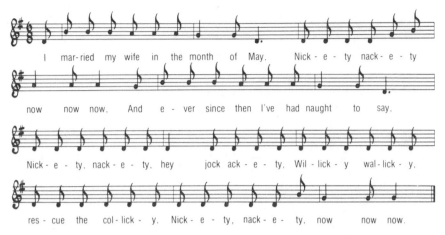

I mar-ried my wife in the month of May, Nick - e - ty nack - e - ty
now now now. And e - ver since then I've had naught to say,
Nick - e - ty, nack - e - ty, hey jock ack - e - ty, Wil - lick - y wal - lick - y,
res - cue the col - lick - y, Nick - e - ty, nack - e - ty, now now now.

I married my wife in the month of May,
    Nickety, nackety, now now now,
And ever since then I've had naught to say,
    Nickety nackety, hey jock ackety,
    Willicky wallicky, rescue the collicky,
    Nickety, nackety, now now now.

She baked a pie and called it mince,
    Nickety, nackety, now now now,
I've never known such misery since,
    Nickety nackety, hey jock ackety,
    Willicky wallicky, rescue the collicky,
    Nickety, nackety, now now now.

She rides to town on the old grey mule ...
And when she does she looks like a fool ...

The halter and bridle they lie on the shelf ...
If you want any more you can sing it yourself ...

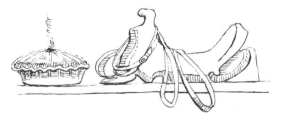

## 200. *There is a Lady in this Town*

There is a lady in this town That loves her husband well. And there's a-no-ther man in the town That she loves twice as well. With a ri - fa-la - fa-lul- lu- ry- um, Sing fa - la - la- loo - ra - lay. With a

There is a lady in this town
That loves her husband well,
And there's another man in the town
That she loves twice as well.

REFRAIN:

With a ri-fa-la fa-lul-ury-um,
Sing fa-la-la-loora-lay,
With a ri-fa-la fa-lul-ury-um,
Sing fa-la-la-loora-lay.

She went to the doctor
To see what she could find,
To try and get some medicine
To run her old man blind.

He gave to her some medicine
And sealed it with his hand
To give to her old man
That he might understand.

She gave to him the medicine
And told him, "Drink it all."

Said he, "I am so blind now
That I can't see you at all."

Said he, "I'd go and drown myself
If I but knew the way."
Said she, "My dearest husband,
You shan't be led astray."

She took him to the waterside,
She took him to the brim.
Said he, "I will not drown myself
Unless you shove me in."

Now she took to her a running jump
To shove the old man in,
But so nimbly he stepped aside
And she went headlong in.

Now my song is finished,
And I cannot sing no more,
But wasn't she the darndest fool
She didn't swim ashore?

## Sources and References

This section identifies the sources for each item and the date it was collected, followed by references to other books containing similar texts. The items were collected in Toronto unless another place is named. The date and place where informants learned some items have been added in parentheses. Those that came from Grade Three pupils in Toronto schools are identified by the name of the school. A few come from a series of weekly articles, "Play Rhymes of the Dominion," that appeared in the Toronto *Globe* between November 13 and December 18, 1909, and a few from students in my folklore class at York University.

Similar rhymes or songs found in other collections are indicated by the names of the collectors or editors whose books appear in the bibliography. When more than one book by the same author is listed, the title is indicated by a key word (e.g., Creighton, *Lunenburg*, 104 refers to page 104 in Helen Creighton's *Folklore of Lunenburg County*). Roman numerals refer to volume numbers, arabic numerals to page numbers (e.g., Randolph III, 141 refers to page 141 in volume III of Vance Randolph's *Ozark Folksongs*).

Because some items are very common, I have not tried to give complete references but have cited only the more important collections of similar material. Wherever possible I have tried to give other Canadian sources, and at least one English and one American reference. I have cited items in magazine articles only where book references were lacking. In general, the number of references is in proportion to the age and popularity of the song or rhyme.

## ROUNDS

**1.** THREE BLIND MICE. Frank Fowke, 1970 (Sask., c. 1918). Cf. Baring-Gould, 156; Best, 114; *Canadian Boys*, 185; Opie, *Dictionary*, 306; Williams, 297; Woodgate, 115.

**2.** ROW, ROW, ROW YOUR BOAT. William Burgess School, 1960. Cf. Best, 113; *Canadian Boys*, 183.

**3.** FRERE JACQUES. Saskatchewan summer camps, c. 1930. Cf. Best, 113; *Canadian Boys*, 119; *Many Nations*, 33; Woodgate, 20.

**4.** O HOW LOVELY IS THE EVENING. As above. Cf. Best, 114; *Canadian Boys*, 182; Cohen, 109.

**5.** O HARK, I HEAR THOSE PEALING BELLS. Mrs. Isabel Smaller, 1961 (Owen Sound, Ont., c. 1916).

**6.** MERRILY, MERRILY GREET THE MORN. As above. Cf. *Canadian Boys*, 182; Woodgate, 141.

**7.** WHITE CORAL BELLS. East York Children, 1959. Cf. Best, 114; Cohen, 104.

**8.** SCOTLAND'S BURNING. Mrs. Isabel Smaller, 1961 (Owen Sound, c. 1916). Cf. Best, 114; Brown III, 197; *Canadian Boys*, 181; Daiken, 102.

**9.** FIRE'S BURNING. East York children, 1959.

**10.** HEY, HO, NOBODY HOME. Bill White, Agincourt, Ont., 1970. Cf. Abrahams, 64; Best, 113; *Many Nations*, 43.

**11.** TO OPE THEIR TRUNKS. Mrs. Isabel Smaller, 1961 (Owen Sound, c. 1916). Cf. *Many Nations*, 26.

**12.** FOLLOW, FOLLOW. As above. Cf. Best, 113; Cohen, 108; Williams, 298; Woodgate, 7.

**13.** RHEUMATISM, RHEUMATISM. As above. Cf. *Canadian Boys*, 119; Turner, 102.

**14.** TURN AGAIN, WHITTINGTON. As above. Cf. *Canadian Boys*, 186; Woodgate, 80.

**15.** SWEETLY SINGS THE DONKEY. Alice Kane, 1970 (Saint John, N.B., c. 1920). Cf. Best, 114; Opie, *Lore*, 176.

**16.** GRASSHOPPERS THREE. Marianne Webb, Don Mills, Ont., 1970. Cf. *Many Nations*, 15.

**17.** WHITE SAND AND GREY SAND. Alice Kane, 1970 (Saint John, N.B., c. 1920). Cf. Cohen, 104; Woodgate, 17.

**18.** MY AUNT HAS A LAME TAME CRANE. Jarvis McCurdy, 1970 (Toronto, c. 1920). Cf. *Canadian Boys*, 183; Cohen, 105; Emrich, 205; Woodgate, 137.

**19.** MY PADDLE'S KEEN AND BRIGHT. Austin Anderson, Winnipeg, 1966. Cf. Cohen, 106; *Many Nations*, 37.

**20.** MAN'S LIFE. Bill White, Agincourt, Ont., 1970. Cf. *Canadian Boys*, 182.

**21.** ALL THINGS ON EARTH. Kate Gardner, 1970.

## Riddles in Rhyme

**22.** LITTLE NANCY ETTICOAT. Alice Kane, 1962 (Saint John, N.B., c. 1920). Cf. Baring-Gould, 275; Brown I, 295; Creighton, *Lunenburg*, 116; Emrich, 13; Daiken, 181; Fauset, 156; Opie, *Dictionary*, 326; Opie, *Lore*, 77; Taylor, No. 608.

**23.** DAFFYDOWNDILLY. As above. Cf. Baring-Gould, 183; Opie, *Dictionary*, 141; Taylor, No. 652.

**24.** RIDDLE ME, RIDDLE ME. Jim Tait, from Toronto children, 1962. Cf. Baring-Gould, 276; Emrich, 43; Fauset, 154; Opie, *Dictionary*, 363; Taylor, No. 640.

**25.** IN SPRING I AM GAY. Karen Hamilton, from Mrs. P. Carroll, Montreal, 1974. Cf. Baring-Gould, 280; Emrich, 24; Taylor, No. 587.

**26.** OLD LADY TWITCHETT. Timy Baranoff, Austin, Texas, 1963 (Toronto, 1930s). Cf. Baring-Gould, 273; Brown I, 294; Emrich, 43; Fauset, 159; Opie, *Dictionary*, 323; Taylor, No. 533.

27. I HAVE A LITTLE SISTER. Alice Kane, 1962 (Saint John, N.B., c. 1920). Cf. Baring-Gould, 274; Emrich, 40; Fauset, 166; Opie, *Dictionary*, 346; Taylor, No. 525; Wood, *Mother Goose*, 91.

28. THERE WAS A THING. Margaret Fulton, Lumsden, Sask., 1920s. Cf. Baring-Gould, 270; Emrich, 48; Opie, *Dictionary*, 403; Taylor, No. 90.

29. IN MARBLE HALLS. Timy Baranoff, Austin, Texas (Toronto, 1930s). Cf. Baring-Gould, 270; Brown I, 298; Creighton, *Lunenburg*, 119; Emrich, 27; Fauset, 167; Opie, *Dictionary*, 196; Taylor, No. 1138.

30. A BOX WITHOUT HINGES. Mary Arnott, from Mrs. L. Wilson, Orangeville, Ont., 1974. Cf. Taylor, No. 1137.

31. AS WHITE AS MILK. Karen Hornibrook, from Joan M. Jack, 1974.

32. I MOVE WITHOUT WINGS. Joyce Cowan, from Nick Butt, 1974. Cf. Taylor, No. 356.

33. I HAVE WINGS. Steve Bowman, 1971.

34. I TREMBLE AT ALL BREATHS OF AIR. Dave Ticknor, from Annie Henderson, Portage la Prairie, Man., 1972. Cf. Emrich, 47, Taylor, No. 728.

35. WHAT IS ROUND AS AN ORANGE. Lynne Cuthbert, from Mrs. Bessie Stewart, Midland, Ont., 1974. Cf. Emrich, 44; Fauset, 158; Taylor, No. 1315.

36. ELIZABETH, LIZZIE, BETSY, AND BESS. Margaret Fulton, Lumsden, Sask., 1920s. Cf. Baring-Gould, 277; Opie, *Dictionary*, 158.

37. BROTHERS AND SISTERS HAVE I NONE. Carol LeGrow, from Cecil McCammon, 1974. Cf. Brown I, 310; Emrich, 157.

38. PATCH ON PATCH. Orest Szewchuk, from Mrs. C. Balfour, Willowdale, Ont., 1972. Cf. Opie, *Lore*, 77; Taylor, No. 1438.

39. FOUR STIFF-STANDERS. Cathy Davis, from Lori-Anne Rubin, Willowdale, Ont., 1972. Cf. Brown I, 304; Creighton, *Lunenburg*, 122; Emrich, 19; Fauset, 155;

Opie, *Dictionary*, 397; Taylor, No. 1479.

40. WHAT IS SMALL AT THE BOTTOM. Marie Robinson, from Percy Hoskin, Port Hope, Ont., 1974. Cf. Brown I, 303; Creighton, *Lunenburg*, 116; Emrich, 26; Taylor, No. 1446; Withers, 94.

41. AROUND THE RICK. Marilyn Holder, from Effie Gollins, 1974. Cf. Emrich, 143; Taylor, No. 805.

42. WHAT IS ROUND AS A DISHPAN. Joyce Cowan, from Laura Steer, Yellowgrass, Sask., 1965. Emrich, 41; Taylor, No. 1324.

43. WHAT'S ROUND LIKE AN APPLE. Marilyn Holder, from Evelyn Vance, 1974.

44. MADE LONG AGO. Jane Hutchinson, from Mrs. C. F. Hutchinson, 1973. Cf. Emrich, 39; Fauset, 154; Opie, *Dictionary*, 173; Taylor, No. 1596.

45. ROUND AS AN APPLE, HOLLOW AS A DRUM. Peter Schopfer, from Leo Henry, 1973.

46. ROUND AS AN APPLE, FLAT AS A CHIP. Richard Naster, from Mary McIntosh, Montreal, 1975. Cf. Emrich, 41; Fauset, 158; Taylor, No. 1337.

47. I HAVE A WEE HORSE. Kathleen Maguire, from Sean Maguire, 1975. Cf. Taylor, No. 425.

48. WALK ON THE LIVING. Irene Szklar, from Ron Hines, Sutton, Ont., 1975. Cf. Taylor, No. 834.

49. WHAT HAS A BED. Bernie Beales, from Myles McLellan, Scarborough, Ont., 1973. Cf. Emrich, 45; Taylor, No. 290.

50. WHAT IS IT YOU CAN TOUCH. Wendy Miller, from Mel Goldberg, 1975.

51. A HILL FULL. Alice Kane, 1962 (Saint John, N.B., c. 1920). Cf. Baring-Gould, 278; Brown I, 306; Emrich, 30; Opie, *Dictionary*, 212; Taylor, No. 1643; Wood, *Mother Goose*, 93.

52. COMES IN AT EVERY DOOR. Irene Szklar, from Margaret Fisher, 1975. Cf. Taylor, No. 193.

**53.** TWO HANDS WITHOUT FINGERS. Alice Kane, 1962 (Saint John, N.B., c. 1920). Cf. Taylor, No. 22.

**54.** THIRTY-TWO HORSES. Timy Baranoff, 1963 (Toronto, 1920s). Cf. Baring-Gould, 275; Brown I, 293; Emrich, 31; Fauset, 157; Opie, *Dictionary*, 219; Taylor, No. 503; Withers, 91; Wood, *Mother Goose*, 105.

**55.** FLOUR OF ENGLAND. Alice Kane, 1962 (Saint John, N.B., c. 1920). Cf. Baring-Gould, 273; Emrich, 26, Daiken, 181; Fauset, 149; Opie, *Dictionary*, 161; Taylor, No. 1096.

**56.** MY FIRST IS A CIRCLE. As above.

**57.** WHAT'S IN THE MILL. Timy Baranoff, 1963 (Toronto, 1920s). Cf. Creighton, *Lunenburg*, 119; Fauset, 163; Withers, 96.

**58.** THREE-QUARTERS OF A CROSS. Margaret Fulton, Lumsden, Sask., 1920s. Cf. Baring-Gould, 272; Brown I, 325; Fauset, 166; Opie, *Dictionary*, 137.

**59.** TWO N'S, TWO O'S. As above. Cf. Creighton, *Lunenburg*, 116; Emrich, 57; Fauset, 167.

**60.** ON YONDER HILL. Timy Baranoff, 1963 (Toronto, 1930s). Cf. Emrich, 39; Fauset, 153; Withers, 96.

**61.** DOWN ON A YELLOW MAT. Jim Brown, 1961. Cf. Creighton, *Lunenburg*, 116; Taylor, No. 947.

**62.** IN A GARDEN. Bruce Kirbyson, from Mrs. G. Kirbyson, 1973.

**63.** MY FIRST IS IN WARLOCK. Karen Sprunt, from Mrs. Gordon Sutherland, 1973.

**64.** KING HENRY HAS SET ME FREE. LaRena Clark, 1966. Cf. Brown I, 309; Fauset, 140.

## Animal Fair

**65.** THE ANIMAL FAIR. Mrs. Nancy Takerer, 1963 (Kingston, Ont., 1940s). Cf. Brown III, 219; Douglas, 43; Emrich, 218; Emrich and Korson, 58; Opie, *Lore*, 38; Randolph III, 207; Sandburg, 348; Withers, 36.

**66.** THE TUNE THE OLD COW DIED ON. O. J. Abbott, Hull, Que., 1957. Cf. Cohen, 51; Flanders, 22; Randolph III, 148.

**67.** THE HORSE NAMED NAPOLEON. Nancy Takerer, 1963 (Kingston, Ont., 1940s).

**68.** THE DERBY RAM. Lamont Tilden, 1962 (Harriston, Ont., 1920s). Cf. Baring-Gould, 298; Brown II, 439; Creighton and Senior, 231; Dean-Smith, 63; Emrich and Korson, 28; Flanders, 24; Gardner, 460; Opie, *Dictionary*, 145; Peacock, 10; Randolph I, 398; Reeves, 102; Sharp II, 184; Williams, 43.

**69.** THE WEE LAMBIE. Alice Kane, 1963 (Saint John, N.B., 1920s).

**70.** THE GOAT. Doris Mosdell, 1970 (Toronto, 1920s). Cf. Brown III, 568; Cohen, 22; Peacock, 65.

**71.** MARY HAD A WILLIAM GOAT. Kenneth Peacock, from Joshua Osborne, Seal Cove, Nfld., 1960. Cf. Best, 85; Sandburg, 336.

**72.** THE THREE LITTLE PIGS. Frank Fowke, 1970 (Sask., 1920s). Cf. Lomax, 307.

**73.** THE FOX AND THE GOOSE. Kenneth Peacock, from Mrs. Clara Stevens, Bellburns, Nfld., 1959. Cf. Cox, 474; Creighton and Senior, 248; Emrich and Korson, 29; Flanders and Brown, 119; Gardner, 465; Lomax, 305; Opie, *Dictionary*, 173; Randolph I, 386; Williams, 247.

**74.** THE FOX AND THE GRAPES. Vera Johnson, from Stanley Botting, Naramata, B.C., 1958. Cf. Flanders and Brown, 247.

**75.** THE PRESBYTERIAN CAT. Roy Clifton, Richmond Hill, Ont., 1958. Cf. Ford, 319.

**76.** THE FROG IN THE WELL. Dr. Keppel, 1958, from step-mother, Mrs. Margaret Russell of Canning, N.S. Cf. Barbeau, 35; Baring-Gould, 17; Best, 50; Brown III, 154; Cox, 470; Creighton, *New Brunswick*, 176; Creighton and Senior, 250; Dean-Smith, 67; Emrich and Korson, 3; Flanders and Brown,

Randolph I, 402; Sandburg, 143; Sharp II, 312; Williams, 133; Woodgate, 104.

**77.** MR. RAT AND MISS MOUSE. Mrs. Lotys Murrin, 1964. For references, see No. 77.

**78.** THE LITTLE KITTY. Mr. and Mrs. H. N. Robinson, 1967.

**79.** THE CROCODILE. Mrs. Isabel Smaller, 1963 (North Bay, Ont., 1924).

**80.** THE WHALE. Saskatchewan summer camps, 1920s.

**81.** THE ROARING CROCODILE. Bill Hughey, Peterborough, Ont., 1957. Cf. Barbeau, 17; Creighton, *Nova Scotia*, 122; Creighton and Senior, 230; Dean-Smith, 61; Flanders, 38; Flanders and Brown, 168; Gardner, 469; Lomax, 498.

**82.** GO TELL AUNT ABBIE. Mrs. Isabel Smaller, 1963 (Owen Sound, Ont., c. 1915). Cf. Brown III, 177; Creighton and Senior, 257; Gardner, 466; Randolph II, 347; Sharp II, 345.

**83.** MISTRESS BOND. Bonnie Dobson, 1961. Cf. Baring-Gould, 306; Northall, 389; Opie, *Dictionary*, 91; Woodgate, 42.

**84.** THREE CROWS. Claire McCausland, Grimsby, Ont., 1963. Cf. Botkin, 63; Brown II, 26; Coffin, 46; Creighton and Senior, 21; Flanders and Brown, 129; Leach, 22; Randolph I, 74.

**85.** THREE CRAWS. Carol Wilson, 1963.

**86.** WHO KILLED COCK ROBIN? Mrs. Nellie Webb, 1963, from father, Neil Thompson, Wallacetown, Ont. Cf. Baring-Gould, 36; *Canadian Boys*, 70; Daiken, 131; Ford, 101; Opie, *Dictionary*, 130; Sharp II, 299; Woodgate, 94.

**87.** THE BIRDIES' BALL. Mrs. Isaac Ireland, 1958 (Toronto, c. 1910). Cf. Haynes, 155.

**88.** THE SWAPPING SONG. Mrs. Pat Anderson Paul and Austin Anderson, Winnipeg, 1966. Cf. Baring-Gould, 29; Brown II, 471; Opie, *Dictionary*, 96 and 163; Ritchie, 10; Sharp II, 307; Williams, 48.

## Tongue Twisters

**89.** BETTY BOTTER. Frank Fowke, 1965 (Sask. 1920s). Cf. Baring-Gould, 283; Brown I, 197; Emrich, 203; Emrich and Korson, 114; Fauset, 130; Opie, *Dictionary*, 73; Wood, *Fun*, 50.

**90.** PETER PIPER. George Webster School, 1970. Cf. Baring-Gould, 291; Emrich, 192; Emrich and Korson, 113; Opie, *Dictionary*, 347; Withers, 79.

**91.** HOW MUCH WOOD. George Webster School, 1970. Cf. Baring-Gould, 283; Emrich, 190; Emrich and Korson, 114; Justus, 14; Opie, *Lore*, 301; Randolph IV, 92; Withers, 80; Wood, *Mother Goose*, 3.

**92.** SHE SELLS SEA SHELLS. George Webster School, 1970. Cf. Emrich, 183; Emrich and Korson, 114; Fauset, 136; Withers, 78.

**93.** SWAN SWAM. Vivienne Stenson, 1958. Cf. Baring-Gould, 282; Emrich, 186; Opie, *Dictionary*, 400.

**94.** IF A SHIPSHAPE SHIP. Mrs. Geraldine Sullivan, Lakefield, Ont., 1958 (1930s).

**95.** BILL HAD A BILLBOARD. As above.

**96.** KNOTT WAS NOT IN. As above.

**97.** THREE GREY GEESE. Alice Kane, 1963 (Saint John, N.B., 1920s). Cf. Baring-Gould, 284; Emrich, 187; Withers, 77.

**98.** SHINY SUSY. As above.

**99.** MOSES SUPPOSES. As above. Cf. Baring-Gould, 283; Emrich, 204.

**100.** SEVENTY-SIX SICK SOLDIERS. Mrs. Geraldine Sullivan, Lakefield, Ont., 1958 (1930s).

**101.** THEOPHILUS THISTLE. Vivienne Stenson, 1958. Cf. Emrich, 196; Emrich and Korson, 114.

**102.** WHICH SWITCH ... FOR IPSWICH. As above.

**103.** A SKUNK SAT ON A STUMP. Alice Kane, from Phyllis Embury, Oakville, Ont., 1973. Cf. Emrich, 188.

**104.** BIG FAT HEN. Vicki Landry, from Michelle Monks, 1972.

**105.** ONE OLD OX. Kenneth Haslam, 1967, from father, born in Middlesex, England, 1891. Cf. Emrich, 208.

## Endless Songs

**106.** MICHAEL FINNIGIN. Saskatchewan summer camps, 1920s. Cf. Best, 89; Cohen, 110; Opie, *Lore*, 31; Sutton-Smith, 99; Withers, 68; Wood, *Mother Goose*, 71.

**107.** JOHN JACOB JINGLEHEIMER JONES. Bruce School, 1962. Cf. Best, 73; Cohen, 109.

**108.** SANDY'S MILL. Eileen Bleakney, Ottawa, from J. R. Jackson, Toronto, c. 1890: *Journal of American Folklore*, 31(1918), 158. Cf. Botkin, 158.

**109.** THE RAGMAN AND THE BAGMAN. As above. Cf. Northall, 366.

**110.** MY FATHER GAVE ME. Kenneth Peacock, from Mrs. Mary Ann Galpin, Codroy, Nfld., 1961. Cf. *JEFDSS*, 1(1934), 135.; Opie, *Dictionary*, 157.

**111.** SHE'LL BE COMIN' ROUND THE MOUNTAIN. Vera Johnson, 1964. Cf. Best, 26; Woodgate, 50.

**112.** HOLE IN THE GROUND. Bill White, Agincourt, Ont., 1970. Cf. Barbeau, 29; Brown III, 184; Cohen, 66; Creighton and Senior, 258; Dean-Smith, 112; Emrich and Korson, 16; Gardner, 474; Karpeles, 72; Leach, 268; Newell, 111; Randolph III, 213; Reeves, 211; Ritchie, 18; Sharp II, 201; Williams, 182; Withers, 146.

**113.** THE WILD MAN OF BORNEO. Mary Ford, 1963. Cf. Creighton and Senior, 258; Shaw, 59.

**114.** THE MALLARD. Kenneth Peacock, from Mrs. Mary Ann Galpin, Codroy, Nfld., 1961. Cf. Dean-Smith, 86.

**115.** OLD KING TWINE. Sam Campsall, 1958 (Owen Sound, 1920s). Cf. "Old King

Cole": Barbeau, 27; Baring-Gould, 143; Creighton, *Nova Scotia*, 197; Dean-Smith, 95; Opie, *Dictionary*, 134.

## Charms and Omens

**116.** A RING AROUND THE MOON. Alice Kane, 1963 (N.B., 1920s). Cf. Brown VII, 345; Northall, 463.

**117.** A SUNSHINY SHOWER. As above. Cf. Brown VII, 337; Emrich and Korson, 62; Northall, 464; Withers, 170.

**118.** A MACKEREL SKY. Frank Fowke, 1965 (Sask., 1920s). Cf. Baring-Gould, 203; Emrich and Korson, 61; Northall, 459.

**119.** WHEN IT RAINS BEFORE SEVEN. Alice Kane, 1963 (N.B., 1920s). Cf. Baring-Gould, 206; Brown VII, 239, 244, 339; Justus, 72; Ritchie, 62; Withers, 170.

**120.** RAIN, RAIN, GO TO SPAIN. As above. Cf. Baring-Gould, 205; Daiken, 175; Northall, 333; Opie, *Dictionary*, 361; Opie, *Lore*, 219; Ritchie, 62.

**121.** RAIN, RAIN, GO AWAY. As above. Cf. Emrich, 234; Emrich and Korson, 62; Opie, *Dictionary*, 360; Turner, 82; Withers, 171.

**122.** MARCH WINDS. Joyce Cowan, from Mark Kurshner, 1975. Cf. Emrich and Korson, 64; Withers, 170.

**123.** RED SKY AT NIGHT. Deborah Leader, from Ellen Russell, 1975. Cf. Baring-Gould, 205; Brown I, 465; VII, 226; Ritchie, 62; Turner, 83.

**124.** RAINBOW AT NIGHT. Frank Fowke, 1965 (Sask., 1920s). Cf. Baring-Gould, 203; Creighton, *Lunenburg*, 104; Emrich and Korson, 62; Fauset, 182; Northall, 466; Withers, 169.

**125.** EVENING RED. As above. Cf. Creighton, *Lunenburg*, 104; Fauset, 182; Northall, 459.

**126.** THE WIND FROM THE EAST. Jane Hutchinson, from Mrs. S. V. Hutchinson, 1974. Cf. Emrich and Korson, 64; Justus, 73.

**127.** WHEN THE WIND IS IN THE NORTH. Elinor Kelly, 1963, from her father who grew up in Guelph, Ont. Cf. Baring-Gould, 204; Brown I, 497; Brown VII, 352, 471; Creighton, *Lunenburg*, 102; Emrich and Korson, 64; Fauset, 181; Justus, 73; Northall, 279.

**128.** AS THE DAYS LENGTHEN. Mrs. Nellie Webb, Don Mills, Ont., 1965, from grandmother who lived in Sarnia, Ont. Cf. Baring-Gould, 182; Brown VII, 344; Northall, 476.

**129.** STAR WHITE. Deborah Leader, 1975. Cf. Baring-Gould, 203; Brown I, 182; Brown VII, 190; Emrich and Korson, 88; Withers, 167; Wood, *Mother Goose*, 4.

**130.** SEE A PIN. Rudy Solomon, 1975 (1960s). Cf. Baring-Gould, 95; Brown I, 458; VI, 436; VII, 575; Emrich, 237; Emrich and Korson, 66; Northall, 174; Opie, *Lore*, 224; Ritchie, 64; Turner, 83; Withers, 168.

**131.** ONE CROW, SORROW. Alice Kane, 1963. Cf. Baring-Gould, 211; Fauset, 184; Northall, 167; Opie, *Lore*, 224; Ritchie, 64; Shaw, 73.

**132.** STEP ON A CRACK. As above. Cf. Baring-Gould, 214; Emrich, 237; Opie, *Lore*, 220; Ritchie, 70; Turner, 83; Withers, 171.

**133.** WEAR AT THE TOE. *Globe*, Jan. 8, 1898 (Orillia, Ont.). Cf. Baring-Gould, 213; Brown VI, 448; Creighton, *Lunenburg*, 114; Emrich and Korson, 68; Fauset, 188.

**134.** LUCKY LUCKY WHITE HORSE. Margaret Fulton, Lumsden, Sask., 1920s. Cf. Brown VII, 373.

**135.** ONE I LOVE. As above. Cf. Baring-Gould, 207; Brown I, 180; VI, 623; Emrich, 235; Opie, *Lore*, 331; Withers, 176.

**136.** SNEEZE ON MONDAY. Ruth Osler, 1965. Cf. Baring-Gould, 219; Brown VI, 87; Emrich and Korson, 76; Justus, 80; Withers, 175; Wood, *Mother Goose*, 8.

**137.** FRIDAY'S DREAM. Alice Kane, 1970. Cf. Emrich and Korson, 77; Northall, 163.

**138.** STUB YOUR TOE. *Globe*, May 20, 1911. Cf. Baring-Gould, 214; Withers, 175.

**139.** IF YOU WISH TO LIVE AND THRIVE. Margaret Fulton, Lumsden, Sask., 1920s. Cf. Baring-Gould, 210; Brown VII, 416; Northall, 281; Opie, *Lore*, 220.

**140.** A WHISTLING GIRL. Alice Kane, 1965. Cf. Baring-Gould, 212; Brown VII, 569; Northall, 506; Withers, 171.

**141.** A SWARM OF BEES. Margaret Fulton, Lumsden, Sask., 1920s. Cf. Baring-Gould, 187; Brown I, 368; Brown VII, 435; Emrich and Korson, 55; Northall, 280.

**142.** MONDAY'S CHILD. Denise Roe, 1972 (St. Catharines, Ont., 1960s). Cf. Baring-Gould, 218; Brown VI, 24; Emrich and Korson, 98; Northall, 161; Opie, *Dictionary*, 309; Ritchie, 59.

**143.** SING OUT OF SEASON. Sally Booker, Saint John, N.B., from mother, 1956.

**144.** CHANGE THE NAME. Jane Hutchinson, 1974, from Mrs. S. V. Hutchinson.

**145.** MONDAY FOR HEALTH. *Globe*, Dec. 18, 1909. Cf. Baring-Gould, 218; Brown I, 447; VI, 649; Fauset, 200.

**146.** SOMETHING OLD. Alice Kane, 1970. Cf. Baring-Gould, 218; Brown VI, 656; Northall, 163; Ritchie, 64.

**147.** MARRIED IN RED. Mary Moffatt, 1969. Cf. Baring-Gould, 215; Brown I, 443; VI, 653.

## Curious Characters

**148.** THERE WAS A CROOKED MAN. Lotys Murrin, 1964 (Owen Sound, c. 1950). Cf. Baring-Gould, 148; Opie, *Dictionary*, 289; Ritchie, 58.

**149.** BESSY BELL AND MARY GREY. Mrs. Goldenberg, 1962 (Scotland, 1930s). Cf. Baring-Gould, 169; Child No. 201; Coffin, 123; Cox, 134; Opie, *Dictionary*, 71.

**150.** TOMMY AND THE APPLES. O.J. Abbott, Hull, Que., 1960 (England, 1880s).

Cf. *Cyril Tawney Sings Children's Songs from Devon and Cornwall*, Argo ZFB 4; *Bunkhouse and Forecastle Songs of the Northwest* sung by Stanley G. Triggs, Folkways FG 3569.

151. PATSY ON THE RAILROAD. Bruce School, 1962. Cf. Best, 105; Lomax, 20; Sandburg, 356.

152. THE OLD SOLDIER. Lamont Tilden, 1957 (Harriston, Ont., 1920s). Cf. Flanders and Brown, 50; Gardner, 483; Sandburg, 432; Shaw, 105.

153. OLD SETH COON. LaRena Clark, 1964. Usually "Old Zip Coon," with various words. Cf. Brown III, 503; Randolph II, 378.

154. LITTLE BROWN JUG. As above. Cf. Best, 79; Brown III, 62; Dean-Smith, 84; Lomax, 176; Randolph III, 141; Williams, 212.

155. JOHNNY WENT DOWN IN THE BUCKET. Claire McCausland, Grimsby, Ont., 1963. Cf. Randolph III, 160.

156. THREE WISE OLD WOMEN. Mrs. Anne M. Croucher, Montreal, 1958, from father, c. 1900. Cf. Randolph I, 439.

157. THERE ONCE WAS A MAIDEN. Bill Thatcher, Grand Rapids, Mich., 1964, from grandmother who lived in western Ontario.

158. MAVERICK, THE TWO-GUN COWBOY. Louch children, Willowdale, Ont., 1963. Cf. Atkinson, 7.

159. A GALLANT SHIP. As above.

160. A LEG OF MUTTON WENT OVER TO FRANCE. Kenneth Peacock, from George Reid, Codroy, Nfld., 1960. Cf. Opie, *Dictionary*, 312; Reeves, 69.

161. THE RICH MAN AND THE POOR MAN. Saskatchewan summer camps, 1930s. Cf. Cohen, 130.

162. OLD ADAM. Frank Fowke, 1970 (Saskatchewan, 1920s). Cf. Sandburg, 39.

163. I WAS BORN FOUR THOUSAND YEARS AGO. Lamont Tilden, 1962. Cf. Best, 70; Brown III, 512; Gardner, 448; Randolph III, 144; Sandburg, 330.

## Dopey Ditties

164. GOODNIGHT, SLEEP TIGHT. Claire McCausland, Grimsby, Ont., 1963. Cf. Emrich, 235; Emrich and Korson, 58.

165. A PEANUT SAT ON A RAILWAY TRACK. P. J. Thomas, from Vancouver children, 1964. Cf. Sutton-Smith, 72; Turner, 101.

166. ONE FINE NIGHT. Catharine Potts and Judy Crawford, 1960.

167. ONE BRIGHT MORNING. Vicki Landry, from Ricky Skybinder, 1972. Cf. Abrahams, 146; Opie, *Lore*, 25; Turner, 100; Withers, 185.

168. I HAVE A LITTLE BROWN COW. Elinor Kelly, 1970, from father who came from Guelph, Ont.

169. THERE IS A BOARDING SCHOOL. Alice Kane, 1970 (Saint John, N.B., 1920s). Cf. Randolph III, 479; Ritchie, 42.

170. O HELL, O HELL. As above.

171. YOU'VE GOT BATS IN YOUR BELFRY. As above.

172. IF-ICKY. As above.

173. SUFFOCATION. Jane Webb, Don Mills, Ont., 1970.

174. AN AWFUL BLACK EYE. Mrs. Isabel Smaller, from David Voyne, Downsview, Ont., 1964.

175. THE HEARSE SONG. Saskatchewan summer camps, 1930s. Cf. Best, 61; Opie, *Lore*, 33; Sandburg, 44.

## Answer-Back Songs

176. BILLY BOY. Mrs. Arlington Fraser, Lancaster, Ont., 1962. Cf. Baring-Gould, 167; Bronson I, 226; Brown III, 166; *Canadian Boys*, 208; Cox, 484; Creighton and Senior, 236; Dean-Smith, 90; Emrich and Korson, 27; Lomax, 320; Opie, *Dictionary*, 78; Randolph I, 391; Reeves, 75; Sharp II, 38; Woodgate, 164.

**177.** MY BOY WILLIE. Lamont Tilden, 1962 (Harriston, Ont., 1920s). References, as above.

**178.** HENERY, MY BOY. Mrs. Nellie Webb, from Vicki Brandon, Clinton, Ont., 1962. Children's version of "Lord Randall." Cf. Bronson I, 191; Child No. 12; Coffin, 36; Dean-Smith, 85; Opie, *Dictionary*, 75.

**179.** A PAPER OF PINS. Mrs. Ethel Minifie, Peterborough, Ont., 1957 (c. 1910). Cf. Baring-Gould, 166; Brown III, 9; Dean-Smith, 82; Emrich and Korson, 14; Gardner, 428; Gomme II, 450; Flanders and Brown, 160; Lomax, 323; Newell, 51; Peacock, 22; Randolph III, 40; Sharp II, 45; Williams, 80.

**180.** WHERE ARE YOU GOING, MY PRETTY MAID? Janet Armstrong, Guelph, Ont., 1957 (1890s). Cf. Brown III, 21; Creighton, *New Brunswick*, 104; Cox, 392; Ford, 127; Greenleaf, 158; Opie, *Dictionary*, 281; Randolph I, 330.

**181.** NO, SIR. Mrs. Arlington Fraser, Lancaster, Ont., 1962. Cf. Botkin, 356; Brown III, 25; Dean-Smith, 93; Newell, 94; Randolph I, 104.

**182.** SOLDIER, SOLDIER, WILL YOU MARRY ME? Claire McCausland, Grimsby, Ont., 1963. Cf. Brown III, 15; Cox, 467; Creighton and Senior, 254; Emrich and Korson, 7; Flanders and Brown, 61; Karpeles, 140; Newell, 93; Randolph I, 289; Sharp II, 40; Woodgate, 78.

**183.** MADAM, I HAVE COME TO COURT. LaRena Clark, 1964. Cf. Brown III, 10; Randolph III, 53; Sharp II, 249.

**184.** MADAM, I HAVE COME A-COURTING. Mrs. Arlington Fraser, Lancaster, Ont., 1961. Cf. Baring-Gould, 168; Creighton, *Maritime*, 121; Newell, 55; Reeves, 163.

## Love ... and Marriage

**185.** LAVENDER'S BLUE. Lamont Tilden, 1962 (Harriston, Ont., 1920s). Cf. Baring-Gould, 113; Dean-Smith, 83; Newell, 120; Northall, 545; Opie, *Dictionary*, 265; Woodgate, 12.

**186.** JOHNNY'S SO LONG AT THE FAIR. As above. Cf. Baring-Gould, 118; Brown III, 170; Creighton, *New Brunswick*, 179; Opie, *Dictionary*, 248; Williams, 201.

**187.** NEW RIVER TRAIN. As above. Cf. Brown III, 137; Lomax, 158.

**188.** RATTLE ON THE STOVEPIPE. Mrs. LaRena Clark, 1964 (northern Ontario, 1930s).

**189.** I TOOK A NOTION NOW. Mrs. Arlington Fraser, Lancaster, Ont., 1962. Cf. Emrich and Korson, 10; Randolph III, 77; Sharp II, 159. (Usually mother and daughter.)

**190.** COMMON BILL. Janet Armstrong, Guelph, Ont., 1957 (1890s). Cf. Brown II, 469; Dean-Smith, 76; Gardner, 430; Lomax, 325; Randolph I, 427; Sandburg, 62.

**191.** MY GRANDMA. Edith Ferguson, 1963 (St. Elmo, Ont., c. 1915). Cf. Brown II, 467; Cox, 469; Creighton, *Maritime*, 36; Dean-Smith, 70; Mackenzie, 379; Randolph I, 383; Williams, 74.

**192.** TYING APPLES ON A LILAC TREE. John Leahy, Douro, Ont., 1962. Resembles a Danish song, "Roselil," in which the suitor ties gold rings on the trees.

**193.** THE BONNY WEE WINDOW. O. J. Abbott, Hull, Que., 1957. Cf. Creighton, *New Brunswick*, 162; Laws, 234 (O18); Randolph I, 431.

**194.** THE GREY MARE. Michael Cuddihey, Low, Que., 1957. Cf. Creighton, *New Brunswick*, 169; Dean-Smith, 71; Gardner, 392; Greenleaf, 59; Laws, 251 (P8); Manny, 281; Peacock, 278.

**195.** THE OLD MAN IN THE WOOD. Mrs. Isaac Ireland, 1958 (c. 1910). Cf. Brown II, 445; Cox, 455; Dean-Smith, 95 (The Old Man and His Wife); Gardner, 415; Justus, 28; Laws, 273 (Q1); Ritchie, 54; Randolph I, 318.

**196.** I WISH I WAS SINGLE AGAIN. Mrs. James Weir, Unionville, Ont., 1957. Cf.

Brown III, 37; Creighton and Senior, 216; Dean-Smith, 96; Lomax, 156; Mackenzie, 347; Randolph III, 66; Sandburg, 47; Shaw, 106; Williams, 111.

**197.** WHEN I WAS SINGLE. Mrs. Nellie Webb, from Mrs. Bovaird, Brockville, Ont., 1962. Cf. Brown III, 54; Lomax, 154.

**198.** DEVILISH MARY. Mrs. LaRena Clark, 1968. Cf. Laws, 275 (Q4), Randolph III, 186; Sharp II, 200.

**199.** NICKETY NACKETY. Mrs. Pat Anderson Paul and Austin Anderson, Winnipeg, 1966. Cf. Baring-Gould, 168; Dean-Smith, 101 (Robin-a-Thrush); Emrich and Korson, 38; Randolph III, 190.

**200.** THERE IS A LADY IN THIS TOWN. Tom Brandon, Peterborough, Ont., 1963 (Fowke, 154; Folk Legacy FSC 10.) Cf. Barbeau, 13; Brown II, 450; Cox, 464; Laws, 274 (Q2); Leach, 282; Peacock, 261; Randolph IV, 248; Reeves, 204.

# Bibliography

Atkinson, Robert M. "Songs Little Girls Sing." *Northwest Folklore*, 2(1967), 2-8.

Abrahams, Roger D. *Jump-Rope Rhymes: A Dictionary.* Austin, Texas: University of Texas Press for the American Folklore Society, 1969.

Barbeau, Marius, Arthur Lismer, and Arthur Bourinot. *Come A-Singing!* Ottawa: National Museum of Canada, 1947.

Baring-Gould, William S. and Ceil. *The Annotated Mother Goose.* New York: Clarkson N. Potter, 1962.

Best, Dick and Beth. *Song Fest.* New York: Oliver Durrell, 1948.

Bleakney, Eileen F. "Folklore from Ottawa and Vicinity." *Journal of American Folklore*, 31(1918), 158-169.

Botkin, B.A. *The American Play-Party Song.* New York: Frederick Ungar, 1937.

Bronson, Bertrand H. *The Traditional Tunes of the Child Ballads.* 4 vols. Princeton, N.J.: Princeton University Press, 1959-1972.

Brown. *The Frank C. Brown Collection of North Carolina Folklore.* 7 vols. Durham, N.C.: Duke University Press, 1952-1964.

Child, Francis James. *The English and Scottish Popular Ballads.* 5 vols. Cambridge, Mass.: Harvard University Press, 1882-1898.

Coffin, Tristram P. *The British Traditional Ballad in North America.* Philadelphia: American Folklore Society, 1950; revised 1963.

Cohen, Mike. *101 Plus 5 Folk Songs for Camp.* New York: Oak Publications, 1966.

Cox, John Harrington. *Folk-Songs of the South.* Cambridge, Mass.: Harvard University Press, 1925.

Creighton, Helen. *Folklore of Lunenburg County, Nova Scotia.* Ottawa: National Museum of Canada, 1950.

Creighton, Helen. *Folksongs from Southern New Brunswick.* Ottawa: National Museums of Canada, 1971.

Creighton, Helen. *Maritime Folk Songs.* East Lansing: Michigan State University Press, and Toronto: Ryerson Press, 1962.

Creighton, Helen. *Songs and Ballads from Nova Scotia.* Toronto: J.M. Dent & Sons, 1932.

Creighton, Helen and Doreen H. Senior. *Traditional Songs from Nova Scotia.* Toronto: Ryerson Press, 1950.

Daiken, Leslie. *Children's Games Throughout the Year.* New York and London: B.T. Batsford, 1949.

Dean-Smith, Margaret. *A Guide to English Folk Song Collections, 1822-1952.* Liverpool: The University Press of Liverpool, in association with the English Folk Dance and Song Society, 1954.

Douglas, Norman. *London Street Games.* London: Chatto and Windus, 1931.

Emrich, Duncan. *The Nonsense Book: of Riddles, Rhymes, Tongue Twisters, Puzzles and Jokes*

Fauset, Arthur Huff. *Folklore from Nova Scotia*. New York: American Folklore Society, 1931.

Flanders, Helen Hartness. *A Garland of Green Mountain Song*. Boston, Mass.: John Worley Company, 1934.

Flanders, Helen Hartness and George Brown. *Vermont Folk-Songs and Ballads*. Brattleboro, Vermont: Stephen Daye Press, 1932.

Ford, Robert. *Children's Rhymes, Children's Games, Children's Songs, Children's Stories: A Book for Bairns and Big Folk*. Paisley, Scotland: A. Gardner, 1904.

Fowke, Edith and Richard Johnston. *More Folk Songs of Canada*. Waterloo, Ont.: Waterloo Music Company, 1967.

Gardner, Emelyn E. and Geraldine J. Chickering. *Ballads and Songs of Southern Michigan*. Ann Arbor: University of Michigan Press, 1939.

Gomme, Alice B. *The Traditional Games of England, Scotland, and Ireland*. 2 vols. London: David Nutt, 1894.

Greenleaf, Elisabeth B. and Grace Y. Mansfield. *Ballads and Sea Songs from Newfoundland*. Cambridge: Harvard University Press, 1933; rpt. New York: Dover, 1964.

Haynes, John C. *Good Old Songs We Used To Sing*, Vol. II. Boston: Ditson Company, 1895.

*JAF, Journal of American Folklore*, 1888—

*JEFDSS. Journal of the English Folk Dance and Song Society*. London, 1932—

Justus, May. *The Complete Peddler's Pack*. Knoxville: University of Tennessee Press, 1957.

Karpeles, Maud. *Folk Songs from Newfoundland*. London: Faber and Faber, 1971.

Laws, G. Malcolm. *American Balladry from British Broadsides*. Philadelphia: American Folklore Society, 1957.

Leach, MacEdward. *Folk Ballads and Songs of the Lower Labrador Coast*. Ottawa: National Museum of Canada, 1965.

Lomax, John and Alan Lomax. *American Ballads and Folk Songs*. New York: Macmillan Company, 1934.

Mackenzie, W. Roy. *Ballads and Sea Songs from Nova Scotia*. Cambridge: Harvard University Press, 1928.

Manny, Louise and James Reginald Wilson. *Songs of Miramichi*. Fredericton, New Brunswick: Brunswick Press, 1968.

Newell, William W. *Games and Songs of American Children*. New York: Harper & Bros., 1903; rpt. New York: Dover, 1963.

Northall, G.F. *English Folk-Rhymes: A Collection of Traditional Verses Relating to Places and Persons, Customs, Superstitions, Etc.* London: K. Paul, French, Trubner, & Co., 1892; rpt. Detroit: Gale, 1968.

Opie, Iona and Peter. *The Lore and Language of Schoolchildren*. Oxford: Clarendon Press, 1959.

Opie, Iona and Peter. *The Oxford Dictionary of Nursery Rhymes*. Oxford: Clarendon Press, 1951.

Peacock, Kenneth. *Songs of the Newfoundland Outports*. 3 vols. Ottawa: National Museum of Canada, 1965.

Randolph, Vance and Floyd C. Shoemaker. *Ozark Folksongs*. 4 vols. Columbia: The State Historical Society of Missouri, 1946-1950.

Reeves, James. *The Idiom of the People*. London: Heinemann, 1958.

Ritchie, James T.R. *The Singing Street*. Edinburgh and London: Oliver & Boyd, 1964.

Sandburg, Carl. *The American Songbag*. New York: Harcourt, Brace and Company, 1927.

Sharp, Cecil J. *English Folk-Songs from the Southern Appalachians*. 2 vols. London: Oxford University Press, 1932.

Shaw, Frank. *You Know Me Anty Nelly? Liverpool Children's Rhymes*. London: Wolfe Publishing Company, 1970.

*Songs for Canadian Boys*. The Quebec Provincial Council of the Boy Scouts Association. Toronto: Macmillan, 1932. (Cited as *Canadian Boys*.)

*Songs of Many Nations*. Delaware, Ohio: Cooperative Recreation Service, n.d. (Cited as *Many Nations*.)

Sutton-Smith, Brian. *The Games of New Zealand Children*. Berkeley and Los Angeles:

University of California Press, 1959.

Taylor, Archer. *English Riddles from Oral Tradition*. Berkeley and Los Angeles: University of California Press, 1951.

Turner, Ian. *Cinderella Dressed in Yella*. New York: Taplinger Publishing Company, 1972.

Williams, Alfred. *Folk Songs of the Upper Thames*. London: Duckworth & Co., 1923.

Withers, Carl. *A Rocket in My Pocket*. New York: Holt, Rinehart and Winston, 1948.

Wood, Ray. *The American Mother Goose*. Philadelphia and New York: J.B. Lippincott, 1938.

Wood, Ray. *Fun in American Folk Rhymes*. Philadelphia and New York: J.B. Lippincott, 1952.

Woodgate, Leslie. *The Puffin Song Book*. London: Penguin Books 1956.

# Index of Titles and First Lines

37318